STOLEN INNOCENCE

Triumphing Over a Childhood Broken By Abuse:

A MEMOIR

ERIN MERRYN

Health Communications, Inc.
Deerfield Beach, Florida

www.hcibooks.com

Out of the respect for their privacy I've changed the names of some of
the people who appear in these pages.

**Library of Congress Cataloging-in-Publication Data
is available from the Library of Congress.**

Publisher: Health Communications, Inc.
            3201 S.W. 15th Street
            Deerfield Beach, FL 33442-8190

R-01-07

Cover design by Andrea Perrine Brower
Inside book design by Dawn Von Strolley Grove

To survivors of abuse and
The Children's Advocacy Center

Contents

Foreword

*"All things work together for good to them that love
God and are called according to his purpose."*

—Romans 8:28

Every two minutes somewhere in America someone is
being sexually assaulted. Ninety-five percent of the time
the victim knows their perpetrator. One out of every sixteen
perpetrators will ever spend time in prison and the ones that
do spend time in prison are usually out in a year or two for
good behavior.

We live in a society where sexual abuse is not a topic to
speak about. With the recent media coverage of the Catholic
priests, it has put a lot of attention on the matter and opened
the eyes of many. It is time people take a hard look at what
our world is coming to. One in every three girls and one
in every six boys will be sexually abused before their
eighteenth birthday. In the United States alone there are an

estimated sixty million survivors of sexual abuse. Sixty-seven percent were abused under the age of thirteen.

A victim of abuse faces a lifetime of humiliating, degrading, and life-altering events. In my diary I give you the personal look into the lives of my family's ordeal and how my innocence and trust were taken from me at a young age. All it took was one night for my entire life to change. Some may wonder why I would expose such a personal and private matter, but if my diary is to save one child from becoming an innocent victim of abuse it was well worth publishing my dairy.

By the time you put this book down you will get an in depth look at my personal journey and how I have become the person I am today. In the time it took you to read this foreword, another person became an innocent victim of sexual abuse.

Acknowledgments

I couldn't have survived the way I have without being blessed by the people in my life.

My parents, who have always supported and believed in me, without your guidance and love I wouldn't be the person I am today! Thank you for the life you have given me.

My sister Caitlin for always being a phone call away. No matter what time of night you were always there to talk giving some of the best advice. You'll go far in life with your dreams.

My sister Allie for her courage of coming forward and being a survivor like myself. We share an incredible bond that will last a lifetime.

The Children's Advocacy Center of Northwest Cook County, Illinois for letting me break my silence and beginning my healing process. You should all be proud of the work you do.

Mrs. Ardell who saw my inner strength. You never doubted me! You've supported me through it all. I wish there were more people in the world like yourself. You'll always have a place in my heart.

Dr. Stern who told me I'd write an incredible book. The countless hours I've spent in your office unraveling my childhood. I wouldn't have done it without your continued support.

Dana and Amanda two people I can always turn to for support or just a good laugh. Thanks for everything you've done over the years.

Kim were both survivors and we will both make the best social workers someday. You're a great friend and although we met on unfortunate circumstances we have come a long way together.

Miss Prokopij who has inspired me to follow in her footsteps of becoming a social worker.

Pastor Bill Hybels for opening my soul and turning me to God. I walk away after your Sunday services with a warm feeling inside.

Finally I owe my biggest thank-you to God. He has been my inspiration and hero. He has been there through the thick and thin never giving up on me.

Even when I doubted him he stuck by my side. I look forward to the day we meet. Thank you!

Introduction

OCTOBER, 2003 8:00 P.M.

I can't believe I still use this little pink diary. I got it so many years ago. Well here are the events of what happened today. Mom pulled into the parking lot of the three-story hospital. Once we got inside we sat down in a waiting room. I sat staring at the large aquarium watching the colorful fish swimming back and forth. What a boring life it must be being a fish. They are so beautiful and seem very peaceful. My life seems to be nothing but the opposite and sometimes there are days I wish I wasn't alive. For a long time I've been searching for peace in my life. I've been sitting on a couch next to my mom as she reads a magazine for the past half hour. Thoughts race through my head of what is to become of me. My nerves are in knots not knowing what is about to take place. A television off to the corner of the room shows the daily news. Why, I wonder, is there nothing but terrible things our world reports in the everyday news? Nothing but murder, rape, and war. I begin to relate to the television as war goes on in Iraq. I'm fighting my own war inside me. I suddenly hear my name being called. A man standing by the receptionist desk introduces himself to me. "Do you want your mom to come with you?" he asks. I told him I would be fine on my own. Mom wishes me good luck as I follow behind the man. Walking down a hallway I notice all the doors are locked and operated from the front desk. I pass a cafeteria and a bunch of offices until I'm led into an office called registration. A middle aged man greets me and asks me a variety of questions. He then goes on to explain how my records are kept confidential. From there I am led to another room where I am told I will have an assessment done. For another twenty minutes, I sit waiting. Looking around, I see another boy about fourteen arguing with his mother. Finally a woman greets me and motions me into a small room. I take a seat on the couch while the woman pulls out papers. She begins by asking me a couple questions. We are interrupted by the sounds of screams and doors slamming outside the room. She tells me we are going to have a code green and it will get pretty loud. She asks me if I wanted to stay there in the room or go back out in the waiting room. I decide to stay where I am. She walked out, closing the door behind her. Over the intercom, I hear code green being called. I then realize the yelling is coming from the boy who was arguing with his mother earlier. The yelling turns to crying as the boy is led away and I assume he is taken to a secure place elsewhere in the hospital. A few moments later the lady apologizes for the trouble and continues. She begins again by asking me what brought me to the behavioral health hospital. I can feel the tears forming in my eyes. I was a victim of sexual abuse.

Innocence

"A child's innocence is priceless."

Author unknown

MAY, 1996 8:00 P.M.

On Wednesday, January 30th, 1985 my mom went into labor. Fifty-seven hours later she gave birth to me at home all naturally on a waterbed. She decided with all her pregnancies not to take any medication for pain. I was twenty-one inches long and eight pounds eight ounces. My parents named me Erin Merryn, pronounced Mur-rin, but my dad's family pronounced it Mare-in. "Erin Mare-in." They thought it was funny. My middle name was changed to Elizabeth a month later. I like Merryn better. As a baby I was very shy and quiet until around two and a half years of age when I started talking and wouldn't stop. I would talk to just about anyone I saw. At three years old a priest told me his name was Father Deimer. I asked him "Whose father?" and he answered me that he was everyone's father, my father, my parents' father, my grandparents' father and even their parents' father! I gave him a funny look and said, "Who are you God?" Everyone got a good laugh especially since it was

3

coming from a three year old. I was considered a daddy's girl
from the start. I'd always be sitting by the door waiting for
daddy to come home. My mom was a stay-at-home mom
raising three girls. I was the middle child. I always enjoyed
my mom's macaroni and cheese, which included a song my
mom made up that we would sing at lunchtime. Dad works
hard running his own business. As a little girl I'd look forward to my kiss, hug, and a high five I received from my dad
before he left for work. My sisters are Allie and Caitlin. Allie
is two years younger then I. Caitlin is the oldest and three
years older than I. My childhood has been filled with trips to
the zoo, amusement parks, beaches, trips to Michigan to
camp and visit the sand dunes. I never had to go far to have
fun. In my own back yard were a swing set, playhouse, and a
huge wooden sandbox my mom made and filled with sand.
My street was filled with children so anyone who drove
down it could hear the screams and laughter of kids. Down
the street lived three boys around my age and they were
friends of Allie and me. Across the street lived Caitlin's best
friend, Carey. The two of them were inseparable. The sidewalks down our street were designed with colorful sidewalk
chalk drawings and the driveways were filled with bikes,
wagons, and strollers. When it was time to leave for school,
the neighborhood kids would meet at our house and my sisters and I would walk with everyone. There was a park down
the street from our house that all the neighborhood kids
would play at. We would also ride our bikes or roller skate in
the tennis court. Summer is the season I've looked forward
to most. Running around the neighborhood barefoot with
my sisters and neighborhood friends. The hot summer days
are always spent in the backyard in the sprinkler or plastic
pool. Most of my weekends are spent in Wisconsin at my
cottage, which my parents bought when I was one year old.

Two years ago I experienced my first big adjustment. WE MOVED! It wasn't far from where I grew up. It is still in the same town and only about five minutes away. The new house backed up to a pond and has a path that leads to the elementary school. Not only did I have to get used to living in a new house, but also a new school. My best friend was moving too, but she was moving all the way to Arizona. Her name was Shannon and I haven't heard from her since I moved two years ago. Although the move was difficult I adjusted well and soon made a new best friend. Her name was Jessica and she was the first one to talk to me when I started my first day at the new school. She was in my class and it was the start of a friendship. The summer after our move we spent most of our time going to our summerhouse and playing at the beach. I also brought Jessica up to Wisconsin where we were dressed in matching red, white, and blue dresses for the annual forth of July parade at the beach. My mom had made the dresses. After a summer of going to the pool, my Wisconsin cottage, fishing in the pond, and the summer day camp run by the park district, it was time for another school year to begin. Another person that came into my life when we moved was Emily. She moved across the street a week after we moved in. So she was new to the neighborhood, too. My sister Allie and I became really good friends with Emily, spending most our time hanging out with her. Early in the school year I learned that Jessica's dad's job was being transferred to Indiana. It was very sad and it was at this time in my life I began to realize that life isn't always fair.

Today I am eleven years old. My mom bought this diary for me at the mall today while shopping with my sisters and me. I live in Illinois and spend a lot of my time in Wisconsin. Both my parents come from large families, but it is my dad's

family that we are close with. They all live very close. My
Aunt Mary and Uncle Scott live just down the path from us.
They have four boys. Jake is their baby. Then there is David,
Mike, and Brian the oldest. Mike is my age and Brian is a
couple years older then I. I sometimes spend more time at
their house than my own since they live so close. My dad
comes from a family of seven kids. So during the holidays it
is a house full of people. At my summer house I spend the
day at the beach, on the boat or in town. At night we do
campfires and roast marshmallows while mom tells ghost
stories. I love watching the sunset or lying under a blanket of
stars in the sky at night. During winter we come to
Wisconsin and either go on our snowmobiles, if there is
enough snow, or go into town and see the ice sculptures. I
also like building snowmen or catching snowflakes with my
tongue.

As far as school goes I am about to finish fourth grade. I
had an awesome teacher this year. Her name is Mrs. Ackman
and she has been the greatest. We just went on our school
field trip to Springfield. We took a coach bus and left at six
in the morning. We saw some interesting places. My favorite
was Lincoln's Memorial. For dinner we stopped and ate at an
Old Country Buffet. I sat with all my friends. We didn't get
home until after ten. My dad had to come get me off the bus
since I'd fallen asleep on the way home. The next day at
school all we did was talk about Springfield and watch
movies. All together it was a fun experience. One I will look
back on for years. I do very well in school except for math. I
struggle with all the equations. I would rather spend my time
daydreaming then learning my multiplication tables.
Reading and writing are my favorite. Well, it is getting late so
I better end this here for the night. I need to get some sleep.
My prayers tonight are for all the sick children who are in

hospitals and aren't fortunate like me to have such a happy and healthy life. Good night!

Erin

JUNE, 1996 4:15 P.M.

It's the last day of school. I am sad because I have made so many new friends this year. One of my very best friends this year was the new girl, Asha. She has very long black hair. Hopefully we will have fifth grade together. I am going to miss Mrs. Ackman, but she told me I have a great teacher for next year. I am excited for summer to spend it going up to Wisconsin. I can't wait to go to the beach. My uncle and dad take my sisters and I along with our cousins tubing. I tend to go very slow because I am terrified of speed. My sister Allie and I bring up our best friend, Emily. Emily is Allie's age, but we both hang out with her. Emily likes to do lemonade stands with us during the summer. We even sell homemade peanut butter cookies that my mom baked. My grandparents also have a summerhouse and condo in Wisconsin. All my other cousins stay at my grandparents' house when they come up. My Aunt Jenny is getting married next month and I'm a flower girl. My sister Allie and our cousin Molly are also flower girls. A bunch of my relatives are flying in from around the country for the wedding. My mom just came in my room and told me to pack my suitcase for Wisconsin. I'll write more later.

Erin

JUNE, 1996 6:20 P.M.

My summer is going good. Today was a fun day. Allie, Emily and I spent the day playing with our dolls. We took them on walks in our strollers to the park and pushed them in the swings. When we came home we played school. I was the teacher and they were my students. We played for a couple hours and then Emily had to go home for dinner. She is coming back later to spend the night. My sister just came in my room to tell me dinner is ready. We are having chicken pot pie, one of my favorites.

Erin

JULY, 1996 10:05 P.M.

Well, my Aunt Jenny got married. It was a fun wedding. Being a flower girl was exciting. There were hundreds of people there. The reception was the best part of the wedding. We did a lot of dancing and didn't get home until really late. It was a night to remember. We later went up to Wisconsin and went over to a house where relatives were renting. We did a bunch of dancing and videotaped the whole party. The fourth of July was also spent in Wisconsin. Our private beach association does a parade each year. We decorate our golf cart and wear our American dresses in the parade. After the parade we eat hotdogs and spend the rest of the day at the beach swimming. Our beach has a slide and a pier that has a diving board and then a raft you have to swim to that has another diving board that is a high diving board. I play a water game with my cousins and sisters called, "rag tag." It is like the game tag, but instead you have a rag you throw at a person. We also play king of the raft and chicken fights on the diving board. So far my summer has been a blast. This week I am having a lemonade stand with Emily and Allie. We are also walking to the store and going shopping together. I'll write more another day. Good night.

Erin

JULY 1996 10:45 P.M.

I'm having such a fun summer. I spent the weekend at the beach and then had a huge campfire at my grandparents' house in Wisconsin with all my cousins. Tonight I went to my Aunt Mary and Uncle Scott's house and while the adults played cards I played in the basement with all my cousins and sisters. We then got into wrestling and I was beating up my older cousin Brian and my other cousin Mike. Brian is stronger than I, but he let me win. We then had foosball tournaments against each other. Allie and Mike went against Brian and me. Brian and I won. We then watched a really scary movie on television until it was time to go home. It was a fun night!

Erin

AUGUST, 1996 12:15 P.M.

Today I went with my family and Uncle Scott, Aunt Mary, and cousins Brian, Mike, David and Jake to Great America. We got there early in the morning. We split up in groups. I stayed with my Aunt Mary and cousins David and Jake because I'm scared of roller coasters. So I spent the day on all the little kid rides, but I had fun. We met up with the rest of the family for lunch at a picnic table. We stayed until it was dark. By then we had to leave because we were driving up to Wisconsin. My sisters slept the whole way home. I sat counting the stars and thinking about how much fun I had all day today. Well it is late so I will end this. Good Night!

Erin

AUGUST, 1996 8:30 P.M.

Today I did so much. First Allie, Emily, and I took our babies for a walk to the park. Then we put the babies to sleep and went fishing in my back yard. We caught a ton of fish. Emily is afraid to take off the fish so Allie and I always have to do it for her. The worst fish to catch are the catfish. They have stingers. We have to use gloves and scissors to get them off. It was a hot and sunny day. I don't think there was a cloud in the sky. It got so hot mom let us turn on the sprinkler in the back yard and we ran around in our swimsuits. I am very tired now so I am going to go to bed.

Sweet dreams!

Erin

AUGUST, 1996 8:05 P.M.

Tomorrow is the first day of school. I will be in fifth grade. I heard my teacher is really nice. I have a bunch of friends from fourth grade in my class. Since today was the last day before school, my Aunt Mary called my mom and we decided to go miniature golfing. My mom, Caitlin and I went. Allie went to Great America with Emily. Aunt Mary had all four boys come with us. We had so much fun. It was a great way to end the summer. After golfing we went out for lunch. Jake eventually needed a nap since he is only two, so we finished lunch and left. I spent a lot of time at my Aunt Mary's house. In fact she told me she is going to need extra help and wanted me to be her babysitter. She knows how much I like babies and little kids. Well it is 8:15 p.m. and I need to get to sleep before my big day of school tomorrow. I'm really excited and happy.

Erin

SEPTEMBER, 1996 10:45 P.M.

I'm really scared and confused right now. Something happened last night, but I don't know whom to tell. My parents stopped over at my grandparents' condo in Wisconsin. When we arrived my cousins were there. Caitlin found out our cousins were staying the night so she asked if the two of us could stay the night. My parents said it was okay as long as we had a ride back home the next day. Our cousin Megan was having her mom pick her up in the morning To take her to the mall and said her mom could take us home. We said goodbye to our parents just as the pizza arrived. We all ate pizza and then the teenagers decided to go walk around the condo, they said I couldn't go with them. I stayed back at the room where Grandma pulled out an air mattress for me to sleep on. I fell asleep while watching a movie. I was expecting to wake from the morning sunlight, but instead woke up around 3:00 a.m. to a very uncomfortable feeling. I felt something moving around in my pants. I immediately realized it was my cousin Brian's hand moving all around my vagina. He was rubbing his hand back and forth. I felt his finger going inside me. I panicked, grabbed his sweaty hand by pulling it out and placing it on his chest. I looked over at him to see his eyes wide open. For a quick second I was looking into his eyes, but then he closed them and pretended to be asleep. I turned so my back was facing him and curled up in a ball. I was sick to my stomach. I could feel the pizza from dinner creeping up my throat as if I were about to puke. For over an hour I lay in fear holding back the tears. Just as the sun was about to rise I fell back asleep. Three hours later I woke up and told myself over and over it was all a dream, but deep in my heart I knew I couldn't fool myself. All morning I couldn't even look at Brian, but at one point we had eye contact and it was one long stare at each other. It disgusted me! I wanted to shower because I felt so dirty. When my aunt arrived she took Megan, Caitlin and me to town for lunch. We went to a place called "Bottles" where they mainly serve pizza. We ordered a cheese pizza, but I couldn't take one bite without feeling like I was going to puke again. Just the thought of eating pizza right now makes me want to throw up. We later went shopping at the mall, but all I wanted to do was go home. I couldn't get last night out of my mind no matter how hard I tried. I just keep telling myself it was a nightmare. I'm really scared and confused. It's been a long day and I need some sleep.

Erin

SEPTEMBER, 1996 9:30 P.M.

It has been three weeks since the situation at my grandparent's condo in Wisconsin. I keep trying to tell myself it was all a dream, but deep down I know it wasn't. I've been babysitting for my Aunt Mary and I see Brian all the time. He acts no different than usual, very friendly and outgoing. I am trying to keep my mind on other things like school, the play I am in, and a book I'm reading. It is hard to stay focused in school and my grades aren't the best right now. When I should be listening to the teacher I'm replaying over in my head what happened three weeks ago. Over time I hope I eventually forget it. It is on my mind so much. It's ripping me apart.

Erin

OCTOBER, 1996 10:15 P.M.

This month has been good so far. I saw my best friend from my old school for the first time in years. It was so great to see her. We went to the park and I learned that it was her birthday. I've also been going shopping and swimming with Emily at the indoor water park by my house. School has been better. I talk to the social worker who comes to my class once a week to talk to me. Well I was thinking of telling him about what happened last month in Wisconsin. I'm just afraid he will tell my parents. We talk about school, my family life, and sometimes play board games. Every time

I try to tell him I panic and leave his office without saying anything. I'm just really scared right now. I went to a family Halloween party last week. My uncle made a haunted house. When it was my time to go in I refused because Brian was one of the people with masks on waiting to scare people and I was afraid he might try something. We also had a pumpkin carving contest and my family won. We had dinner there and left when it was late and everyone was tired. Speaking of tired I am very tired and have school tomorrow. Good night!

Erin

OCTOBER, 1996 10:15 P.M.

I got so much candy tonight. I went trick or treating with some friends and then my mom and dad drove Allie and me around the neighborhood when it got dark so we were safe. I was dressed up like a grandma. I have been dressing up like a grandma since I was in first grade. It is a really good costume. Well I had a lot of sugar tonight so I am wide-awake, but going to put my diary away for now. Night!

Erin

NOVEMBER, 1996 9:45 P.M.

On November 8th we moved into our new summerhouse in Wisconsin. We went from a one-bed room house with a loft upstairs to a seven-bedroom house with a basement. The cottage we moved out of is directly behind us and to the corner. My dad sold it to one of his high school friends. I picked my room out right away. Grandma and Grandpa slept over the first night with us. The house needs some work, but my dad is fast at that. The kitchen has swinging doors and the tile is yellow and red making it look like a McDonald's kitchen. That will all change eventually. We had Thanksgiving at my grandparent's house like every year. It was a good turkey. There was so much food to choose from. My favorite is mashed potatoes and stuffing. The adult guys all watched football. My cousins and I played cards. We came home late and I went right to bed. Christmas will be here before I know it. The first thing on my Christmas list is a dog. I've asked for it every Christmas and birthday. I want either a Labrador or Golden Retriever. I'll write more another day.

Erin

Into the Night

*"Whatever you fear most
has no power—it is your fear
that has the power."*

Author unknown

January, 1997 10:00 P.M.

It is a new year with a new start. I had a great Christmas. We had a holiday village at my school that my mom was in charge of. It was an awesome village. There was singing, dancing, food, shops, photographer, and much more. We made Christmas cookies and listened to Christmas music a day before Christmas Eve. Christmas Eve was spent at our house. All my relatives came over. Every year we draw names for a cousin to buy for. I had my cousin Mike and bought him a harmonica. It was so beautiful out. Christmas morning it snowed and we went for dinner at my Grandparents' house. For New Year's my friend Lauren came to my house in Wisconsin and we did the countdown together. We threw confetti everywhere, which mom later got upset about. It has been a good start to the New Year so far. I've met a new best friend this year named Kristin. We hang out a lot and I plan to invite her to my birthday party. We also have a student teacher in our class now. Her name is Mrs. Day. She is really nice. My birthday is also coming up. I will be twelve years old on February second. Well I have school tomorrow. Good night!

Erin

FEBRUARY, 1997 11:30 P.M.

My birthday party was a blast. I had Emily, Melissa, and Kristin come to my house in Wisconsin for an overnight. We played bingo and won prizes. The next morning we went out for a walk down to the lake. The entire lake is frozen so we decided to walk on it. There were plenty of cars on the ice. Then suddenly a dog came running up to us. We couldn't get him to leave so instead we ran on the ice with the dog. It was so much fun. He followed us all the way home and we gave him a name. We called him Miracle. I wanted to keep him so bad, but my mom told me he has a family that misses him. It was like my wish from blowing out my candles was coming true. We later called the number on the dog's tags and a man with a pick-up truck came shortly after to pick the dog up. Some-day I hope my wish does come true. For now though I will have to keep dreaming. Good night!

Erin

MARCH, 1997 11:30 A.M.

This month has been sad. Mrs. Day is leaving and I have really grown to like her. She gave me her address to write her. Then my friend Kristin got a chocolate Labrador puppy. It was so cute and made me upset that my parents won't let me have a dog. Spring break is almost here and my Aunt Mary wants me to watch David and Jake for her. Brian and

Jeff are too busy with their older guy friends to watch the boys. I really enjoy it though. I stopped over at my Aunt Mary's every day after school. She is always stopping me after school and asking me to help her out. Since our house is on the same path I walk right past it every day before and after school.

Another thing I am dealing with right now is my vision. I have an eye problem that is making me go blind. I see different eye doctors who specialize in my situation. It isn't a fun experience at all. Well, I am going to a garage sale with Allie and Emily, then we are having a sleep over.

Erin

APRIL, 1997 9:35 P.M.

It wasn't a dream. What happened at Grandma and Grandpa's condo seven months ago in fact did happen. It happened again today, but this time I wasn't sleeping. I was fully awake and alert. I'm so scared right now. My eyes are filled with tears and I don't know whom to turn to. I was babysitting Brian's younger brothers David and Jake. My Aunt Mary was going to the store for groceries. She told me she would be gone an hour. I began playing "hide and go seek" with David and Jake like I do most of the time when I baby sit. Brian came home when David was counting. I was about to hide when Brian told me he had an excellent hiding spot. He told me to follow behind him. I didn't think once about what happened in Wisconsin. I tried blocking that all out back when it happened. I followed Brian downstairs to the basement to a door, which brought us to this storage area where you had to crawl. Brian climbed up and then helped me. There was a lot of stored items down there.

Brian grabbed blankets and told me to hide under them. I went under the blankets by myself. About a minute or two later Brian crawled over and was under the blankets with me. I was a little nervous when he got under the blankets. I could hear David upstairs walking around looking for us. Brian slowly started to touch me. I didn't say anything at first, but then he started to get aggressive by putting his mouth on mine and trying to kiss me. I tried pushing him off, but he then just got on top of me and he is twice my size. He lay on top of me and started to touch me. Slipping his hands down my pants and all I wanted to do was cry. Over and over I asked him to please stop. I was terrified and couldn't believe what was happening to me. His hands slipping down my pants and up my shirt. His heart pounding against mine. We then heard David opening the door to the storage area. Brian told me to get quiet. I wanted to scream, but didn't want David to see anything even though it was extremely dark. I don't think David would be able to understand nor see what was happening. I heard David turn around and make his way back upstairs while Brian continued to touch me. It went on until we heard my Aunt Mary's high heels on the tile floor above us coming in. Brian quickly made his way to exit and left me by myself. I came up a few minutes later where I saw David sitting with Jake watching cartoons. David looked at me and said, "Where were you this whole time?" I didn't know what to say so I didn't say anything at all. My Aunt Mary paid me and I walked home. The whole way home I sobbed. Over and over in my head I thought about what just happened. In school once we had a guy called Officer Friendly come in and teach us about stranger danger. Never to answer the door when your parents aren't home. Never talk to strangers. I thought people like Brian jumped out of bushes at night and attacked you. I was never warned about my own family. They don't teach you that in school. At dinner tonight I didn't say much. I was too upset, but tried not to show it. Mom noticed I seemed down and asked what was wrong. I told her it was nothing but she thought it had to do with my eyes.

My vision problems have been getting worse and the doctors say surgery is in the future. I can't even think about that right now. I went straight to my bedroom after dinner and didn't even do my homework. I am laying here on my bed in almost complete darkness except for my night light that gives off enough light for me to write. I don't think I will be getting much sleep tonight. I'm really scared! I just want to wake up from this horrible nightmare. This can't be happening. I feel so alone and confused. I just want it to stop!

Erin

APRIL 1997 11:15 P.M.

This month has been terrible, but my dream for years finally came true. I always wondered how many more birthday candles would I blow out until I had my wish come true. Well my wish finally came true today totally unexpected. I came home from school and found a note that my mom left me stating she went shopping and would be back later. Around 5:30 p.m. I got off the phone with Emily when my mom whistled for me. She asked me to help carry in a few things. When I got outside and walked to the bottom of the stairs and looked up at the car I saw a huge dog sitting in the front seat. I was screaming with excitement and thanking my mom over and over again. Giving her the biggest hug ever. She told me his name was Chance and he was a Labrador retriever. I put the dog on his leash and while mom was putting his metal cage together I ran over to Emily's house to show her. Emily thought I was lying since she knew how much my dad disliked the idea of having a dog. Which got me thinking how did mom convince dad. We walked back over to my house where mom was still in the garage working on the cage and I asked her how she convinced dad. She told me she didn't convince him she did it without his knowledge. Emily and I took the dog down the path over to my Aunt Mary's where Allie went after school. I could see Brian in the kitchen when I walked up the back yard but just avoided looking at him. Through the window I told Allie and she didn't believe me nor did anyone else. They all know how much my dad would never let me get a dog. Allie called home and learned that it was true. When Dad got home he wasn't too happy to see the dog. In fact he pretended he didn't see it at first and walked right past my mom as she set up the cage. My mom decided to get me the dog because of all the problems I was having with my vision. When Caitlin got home tonight I was outside with the dog and she thought I was dog sitting for someone. When I turned to her and said, "Like our new dog." Her mouth dropped and couldn't believe it. It has been a good night! One I will count my lucky stars for. The nights haven't been good in a long time. I am up with nightmares and I cry myself to sleep a lot. I hope this dog helps take away some of my loneliness! Good night!

Erin

JUNE, 1997 8:30 P.M.

June 5th was the last day of school. It was a fun last week. Most of my friends are looking forward to the summer. I'd rather stay in school. I will be babysitting for my Aunt Mary. Brian touched me again last week. I was upstairs with the boys watching them play Nintendo. We were in Brian and Jeff's room. Brian came in and began trying to sit on me. I struggled with him but it was too late. He was on top of me before I knew it. He slowly began slipping his hands down my pants then started going up my shirt and felt my chest. I didn't want to draw attention to what he was doing because the boys were in the room. So I stayed silent hoping it would end soon. I don't know what to do or who to turn to. I'm just really scared right now. It is going to be the summer of hell. Emily is on her way over so I must end this for now.

Erin

JULY, 1997 8:30 A.M.

The Fourth of July parade was fun. We went to dinner with the whole family and watched fireworks. So far this summer I've been swimming, tubing, sleepovers, sitting around campfires, and babysitting. Everything has been good except when I baby-sit. Yesterday I was over at Brian's playing "hide and go seek" with David and Jake. Brian came upstairs and followed me into the bathroom. I then watched him lock the door. I was terrified and knew what was about to happen. The look in Brian's eyes tells it all. It's a look of excitement and determination. I struggled with Brian. Fighting my way to unlock the door. Brian is a lot bigger than me. He is a high school football player with a lot of strength, but I wasn't about to give up without a fight. Brian eventually pushed me into the shower and up against the wall. Forcing his body on me. He began smiling and I could tell he saw the terror in my face. He began to force his hands down my pants. I was screaming for my sister, but she had no idea what was happening. I threatened Brian that I was going to tell on him and he just threatened me back saying no one would believe me. I eventually pushed Brian off me and was able to unlock the door. I walked home immediately after it happened. I want to tell someone, but who is going to believe me? I'm so scared! HELP!

Erin

AUGUST, 1997 9:15 P.M.

It happened again, this time in Brian's bedroom closet. I was upstairs watching the younger boys when I heard Brian come home. I immediately climbed into Brian's closet praying he wouldn't come up stairs looking for me. It was to late. Brian asked the boys if they knew where I was and they told him I had just been in the room. Brian must have known I was hiding because he began roaming the upstairs for me. Brian is like a mountain lion looking for his next attack. Never knowing when he will strike. The younger boys continued to play Nintendo and Brian came back in the room looking. When Brian opened his closet I sat as still as possible, but Brian discovered me. He told me I couldn't outsmart him. He climbed in the closet and closed the door. He slowly began touching me as I begged him to please stop. Slipping his hands down my pants. He ignored my pleas and continued to touch me. His hands so rough and large compared to my tiny hands. I try pushing him away, but it doesn't stop him. Instead he becomes more aggressive. The closet was small so it made it harder to fight Brian off. All I could hear was the sound of the Nintendo game the boys were playing in the room they had no idea what was happening. I honestly think if they did see Brian touching me they wouldn't think anything of it since they are too young to understand. I knew I couldn't fight Brian off so instead I held my breath and closed my eyes hoping it would end soon. He eventually stopped when David and Jake came looking for me. Brian whispered in my ear that if I told anyone they wouldn't believe me. The truth is I am afraid to tell. I feel Brian is right and no one will believe me and I don't want to destroy our family. I'm afraid if I tell I will be in trouble for not telling sooner. I don't know what else to do. All I do is pray. Pray that someone other than myself will hear my pleas for help. I sometimes hope mom will discover my diary and read it.

Erin

SEPTEMBER, 1997 10:00 P.M.

I had a sleepover with Emily this weekend and I asked her if I could tell her a secret if she promised not to tell anyone. I finally told her and she was shocked. She was disgusted especially since she knows Brian. All night she tried convincing me to tell my parents, but I told her I couldn't and if I did no one would believe me. She is the only person who knows what Brian is doing and I trust her not to tell anyone.

Last week my Aunt Mary stopped me after school and asked if I could watch the boys. Like usual I agreed to come over. For some reason I have a hard time saying no to my aunt. I don't know why I just feel bad saying no to her. The boys were in the basement while I was upstairs reading a magazine when I heard someone coming in from the laundry room. Brian appeared from the corner and came into the family room where I was sitting. I tried to stay clam, but Brian could see straight through me and saw the fear in my eyes. I tried to start a conversation with him. Then I saw a bunch of kids from my grade running laps for track outside Brian's house. I realized I forgot I had track practice after school. It isn't mandatory, but I would much rather be there than sitting next to Brian. I asked Brian if he could watch the boys because I was suppose to be out there with the rest of the team. Brian told me I could miss one practice without getting in trouble. I didn't know how to respond to him without upsetting him so I told him my coach would be upset with me for not coming to practice. It was the only thing I could think to say. Brian put his hands on my shoulders as I watched from the window as my classmates ran by. He then slowly started to slip his hands down the back of my pants. While fondling me he continued to talk to me like nothing was going on which confused me even more. When we heard Mike coming in the house Brian stopped and went into the kitchen to get something to eat. My Aunt Mary arrived soon after which is when I left. I just don't know how much more I can take. I am sick of living with this secret. I can't stand going through this. Will it ever stop? Why is he doing this to me? I don't get it!

Erin

SEPTEMBER, 1997 9:45 P.M.

We were invited over for dinner tonight at my Aunt Mary and Uncle Scott's house. After dinner the adults played cards like usual and all the cousins were off playing Nintendo in the basement or watching T.V. I was in the basement with my younger cousins playing in the dark with the lights off. I was under a blanket trying to scare them. We didn't play long because Jake got scared and went upstairs. I continued to play with my sister Allie and cousin David. I felt safe since I knew Brian wasn't home all evening. Suddenly I felt someone hovering over me, but much heavier then David or Allie. Immediately I knew it was Brian. I didn't say a word. Instead I lay on carpeted floors as Brian crawled under. The darkness made it impossible to see him, but the touch of his cold hands rubbing my chest made it clear who it was. He eventually began moving his hands in a slow motion up my chest and down towards my belly button, his other hand grabbing my butt. For some reason my body froze and I didn't fight him off. Once he got off my motionless body I went upstairs and nagged my parents to go home. After trying to convince them for thirty minutes, we finally left. I climbed in bed and cried into my pillow. Feeling so disgusted. I want to go crawl in bed with one of my sisters to feel safe. He lives so close I fear he'll walk over in the middle of the night and come in the house without anyone knowing.

Erin

OCTOBER, 1997 8:45 P.M.

I took my dog on a long walk today. I love my dog so much. Whenever I look into his big brown eyes I sense that he understands my pain. It is almost like he knows what I am going through. I know it sounds crazy, but in a way it is comforting to think that. This year has been tough so far. I have so many things going on in my life. My eyes are continuing to get worse and the doctors are planning a date for surgery. I'm also struggling to do well in school. I do terrible on tests. No matter how hard I study it doesn't show. I continue to struggle in math, so my teacher recommends a tutor to come to my house weekly. She will just work with me on math skills and prepare me for tests. Speaking of math I have math homework to finish so I better end this entry.

Erin

OCTOBER, 1997 1:20 A.M.

I'm rocking back and forth. I am so afraid to go to sleep because all I do is have nightmares of Brian on top of me. It is after one in the morning and I have school tomorrow. Today Brian touched me again. Allie and I were over at Brian's house playing in the basement with the younger boys. Brian came down with a friend and began playing tickle monster. He goes under a blanket and with all the lights off trying to find us and tickle us. Well, I knew what he was planning on doing so I got in the corner of the basement and stayed as quiet as I could hoping he wouldn't find me. My plan was to get upstairs without Brian seeing me, but it didn't work out the way I hoped it would. Brian stopped me before I got to the stairs and pulled me under the blankets and began touching me. I was able to free myself and run to the couch. He then went after his brother trying not to draw so much attention to me. Within a few minutes though he was back on top of me under the blankets. This time I was lying on the couch. There was nothing I could do so I buried my head in the cushions and prayed he'd get off me. I heard my sister and the younger boys run upstairs where Brian's friend was. I didn't understand why they were leaving. I screamed for them to save me, but they thought I was just having fun. They all really didn't know what was happening under the blankets. If only they knew. Brian's hands started to move rapidly all over my chest, at times reaching down and grabbing my butt. Eventually he'd get one of his hands down my pants and gently rub my vagina while breathing heavily into my ear. Brian finally let me go after about fifteen minutes of not saying anything. All I did was hide my head from looking him in the face. He looks like a crazy man on a mission when he is abusing me. I'm afraid of the dark at night because all I see are images of Brian coming towards me. I have to leave my bedroom door open and a night-light on at night just to fall asleep. I just wish it would all end. I need to try and get some sleep since I have school tomorrow and an eye doctor appointment. God hold me tonight. Keep me safe. Please protect me from my cousin.

Erin

NOVEMBER, 1997 5:30 P.M.

Emily spent the night last night. We went to the mall all day today. I'm trying to avoid babysitting for my Aunt Mary. It seems no matter how hard I try to stay away from Brian he always seems to appear. Thanksgiving and Christmas are coming up and I can't even get excited. All the holidays mean to me are another day trying to avoid Brian. Well Chance is crying to be walked so I better go walk him.

Erin

NOVEMBER, 1997 11:35 P.M.

It is Thanksgiving night and it happened again. I can't stop crying tonight. Everyone is asleep in my house on a full belly of turkey except me. Things were going good tonight, I had turkey, stuffing, mashed potatoes and my mom's yummy pumpkin pie. After we ate, I played with a bunch of my cousins in my grandparents' garage. The garage is more like a playroom. It is carpeted and is filled with a bunch of different items. I was playing house and I was the mom to all my younger cousins, Allie was playing, too. I had my back to the door and never saw Brian open it. I immediately went to hide hoping he wouldn't see me. Brian came in and I heard him ask my sister and the other cousins if they wanted to play tickle monster. They all wanted to so Brian turned off the lights and crawled his way around. He decided not to use a blanket. I was in the corner hoping he didn't know I was in there. Unfortunately he did and came directly to my corner and began reaching his hands down my underwear. I was in the dark and all I could see was a little light from the other end of the garage where the door was that entered into the laundry room and then into the kitchen where all my relatives were. My sister Allie and cousin David were in the garage hiding, too. Brian didn't want to draw attention only to me so after five minutes of touching me he went for the other cousins. That is when I tried to make my escape, but he grabbed my ankle just before I reached the door and forced me into the back of the garage where he began touching me all over. Eventually after ten more minutes went by Brian let go of me and walked out of the garage into the family room to watch football. When I finally climbed out of the garage, all I wanted was to go home and go to sleep. I'm finally home and don't know how much longer I can stay silent. I feel so alone and lost. I just want someone to hold me and never let go. My tears are making my eyes blurry and making the ink run on this entry. I'll end it here.

Erin

DECEMBER, 1997 3:00 P.M.

Christmas is in a couple weeks, but I'm not excited at all. All Christmas is for me is being terrified of Brian. Trying to escape his power. Seriously, what am I supposed to do? I'm in my closet right now as I write this. If I could ask for anything for Christmas there would be two things I'd ask for. One being that Brian would never lay a hand on me again. The other being that my vision would get better. I'm legally blind in one eye and the doctors are planning surgery for summer time. I just want things to be easier for me. Well, Allie wants me to watch Christmas movies with her and have hot cocoa. Maybe it will help get my mind off things for a while. I'll let you know how Christmas goes.

Erin

DECEMBER, 1997 6:15 P.M.

I got some great stuff for Christmas, but once again I tried avoiding Brian. We all went to my aunt's for Christmas Eve. I stayed around adults most of the night. At one point I had to use the bathroom. The bathroom on the ground floor was being used so I went upstairs to use the other bathroom. When I came out I heard my cousins in one of the bedrooms. I decided to stay up there and play with the rest of them. Eventually one by one we all started to go down stairs. Brian stood at the top of the stairs trying to prevent me from coming down. I was trapped. My other cousins thought he was just playing with me. When I tried to push him out of the way, he turned to me and said, " Don't make a scene and just listen to what I have to say." I made a mad dash for a bedroom where I tried to close and lock the door. I tried holding it with all my strength, but Brian had no problem getting it open. He quickly closed it and locked the door. The room was tiny and dark. The only light came from a small night light on a table. Brian stood against the door watching me pace back and forth. My mind was racing not knowing what was going to happen. I tried not to act scared, but Brian could hear the tremble in my voice when I tried talking to him. Talking to him was useless. He could care less what I had to say, but every minute counts when he has me trapped. The longer I can keep him away the less time I will be stuck with him. All he wanted was to terrorize me and find his chance to hurt me.

I walked over to the window and looked out at the full moon and stars. I began praying to God that he would save me from Brian. While I said a silent prayer Brian stood against the locked door watching my every move. I could feel the vibration from the floor from the rest of my relatives downstairs celebrating Christmas Eve. Just when I was about to lose all hope and Brian was moving in close to make his move, there was a knock at the door that startled both of us.

Brian unlocked the door to see my Uncle John standing there. Our Uncle John questioned what we were doing, but really didn't care. The reason he came up was to find a tape of haunted ghost stories. My Uncle John called all the cousins upstairs to sit in the dark and listen to the tape. I really wasn't interested, especially since it was Christmas not Halloween, but at that point I'd do anything to be away from Brian. My cousins all gathered on the floor in the tiny bedroom and listened to the tape. As I listened I felt something slipping down my pants. I then realized it was Brian sitting directly behind me doing what he had planned to do before. I immediately hit his hand and then jumped up, opened the door and made my way downstairs. I was no longer looking forward to presents, but instead getting home to my own bed where Brian couldn't hurt me. My parents leave early every Christmas Eve because tradition in our home was opening presents on Christmas Eve. Mom and Dad would put all the presents under the tree. Every year my sisters and I ask for a trampoline, but never received one. Dad feels they are too dangerous and doesn't want any accidents. A relative always drives my sisters and me home later, giving my parents time to put the presents down. This year it was Brian's parents driving us home.

When it was time to go I was the last one to get in the car. There were three people in the front seat including a car seat for Jake. The only place for me to sit was in the back. There wasn't any room back there either. Caitlin, Brian, and Jeff were all sitting back there so the only option was for me to sit on someone's lap. Brian immediately offered and although I didn't want to at all Brian was giving me a dirty glare. For thirty minutes I was stuck sitting on Brian's lap the whole way home. Brian used his hands to rub my butt. I did my best to ignore it, but deep down I couldn't take it. To keep my mind off it, I talked about getting a trampoline. When I finally saw my street sign, I was relieved. My sisters and I darted inside as my Aunt Mary yelled out the window for us to call her in the morning. We opened up our presents, but it wasn't the same as years past. Brian's actions were really beginning to affect me. I'm twelve years old and can't even enjoy the Christmas holiday. Instead I'm worried about my safety and keeping this terrible secret that is eating away inside me.

After opening presents my sisters and I ran downstairs to our stockings. To our surprise there was a huge box and on it printed in bold letters was the word Trampoline. My sisters and I were jumping up and down and screaming with excitement. For a moment I actually forgot about my troubles and felt like a kid opening presents. My sisters and I stayed up late into the night and eventually we all crashed in Caitlin's room. We woke around seven thirty this Christmas morning. Grandma and Grandpa stopped over later to see our presents. Around three p.m. we all went over to our Grandparents' house for Christmas dinner. Once again I worried about Brian trying to hurt me. I stayed by my parents' side all night, which kept Brian from abusing me. Christmas night I came home and cried myself to sleep holding my teddy bear. I was just glad to have another holiday behind me.

We are leaving for Wisconsin now. We are spending the New Year in our new house. Mom told me today that Aunt Mary and Uncle Scott are coming with the boys for the New Year. It has only been four days since Christmas and once again I must face Brian. All I can do is pray. Pray Brian will not hurt me since I don't have the strength to fight him off.

Erin

Breaking My Silence

*"No person is your friend who demands
your silence, or denies your right to grow!"*
—Alice Walker

JANUARY, 1998 9:30 P.M.

It is a new year and a new start on life. New Year's was fun. I stayed near my sisters most of the night and we played cards and board games. After ringing in the New Year, my sister Caitlin, three of my cousins, and I decided to walk around the neighborhood. Brian was one cousin who came with us. It was very dark out, but not very cold for winter. We walked down the street and saw a house with the TV going like they had just watched the count down. The plan was that someone would knock on the door and then everyone else would moon the person who answered the door and scream Happy New Year. I wasn't thrilled about the idea so I offered to knock. After knocking a man didn't come to the door, but instead he looked out the window where Brian, Caitlin, Mike, and Megan mooned the man and we all took off running. We were gone about an hour when we finally came back home. My dad was on the phone when we got back which I found odd for one in the morning. I later learned my dad's uncle died. His uncle was celebrating the New Year when he collapsed and later died of a heart attack. Well, Brian stayed away from me tonight and later left that night with the rest of his family. One more holiday out of the way.

Erin

JANUARY, 1998 9:30 A.M.

Today my cousins on my mom's side of the family are coming to our house. They are from Michigan. We have plans to go shopping at the mall and go to the movies. We are also going to go swimming at our local indoor pool. My cousins are close in age with me. Kelly is a year older and Gina is six months younger. So I get along with both of them. Anyway I must clean my room before they get here.

Erin

JANUARY, 1998 10:30 A.M.

My cousins left this morning after spending two days with us. I spent most my time hanging out with Kelly. Last night Kelly slept in my room. I began asking her if she had any secrets. I told her that I needed her to promise me that I could trust her if I told her a secret. I knew I could trust her and began telling her about Brian. She was disgusted and couldn't believe it. We stayed up really late talking. Then this morning while my cousins were packing to go back to Michigan, the phone rang. My mom came upstairs a few minutes later and told us we were going to Aunt Mary's for dinner and cake to celebrate Grandpa's birthday. My stomach turned to knots and I didn't feel well. Kelly turned to me when no one was around and asked if that was Brian's house. I told her it was and Kelly made me promise to stay as far away from Brian as possible. Don't let him hurt you any more is what she told me. She gave me a big hug and wished me luck. When I waved good-bye she said she would be praying for me. It has been about an hour since they left and I'm sad they had to go. Kelly cared about me and being able to talk to her made me feel better. Now I must prepare myself for tonight. School also starts tomorrow after our two-week winter break. I'm going to go have a bowl of cereal and watch some television. I'll write more tonight when we get home.

Erin

JANUARY, 1998 11:45 P.M.

I tried so hard to outsmart Brian, but the truth is he outsmarted me instead. I am in so much pain right now. He really hurt me. Most of the night I stayed by my mom's side or in the kitchen where a lot of action was going on. Brian came in and out of the kitchen, but eventually I saw him leave out the front door and walk over to his friend's house. I could finally escape his control. I went upstairs and began playing with David, Jake, Allie, and my other cousin Molly.

We were playing a board game. I was Jake's partner because he needed help. After playing for about fifteen minutes we heard they were about to have cake. While Allie and the boys went downstairs, I finished picking up the pieces and put the board game away. Just as I was turning off the light in David and Jake's room, Brian appeared at the door. My heart began to pound and my palms started to feel sweaty. I tried to show as little fear as possible. I began to walk down the hallway towards the stairs when Brian stopped me and pushed me into his room. There wasn't a light on so I was forced to struggle in the dark. Brian's nickname for me was psycho because of how long I would fight with him and would always lose. I told him over and over to leave me alone and all he does is laugh. He acts as if what he is doing is normal. Brian forced me over to the corner of the room and onto a green bean bag chair. I was filled with so much anger that once again Brian fooled me and I fell in his trap. With the door closed and the lights were off, Brian sat next to me and began to slowly move his hands down the front of my pants. I knew no matter what I couldn't fight Brian off. Instead I just lay there in silence holding back my tears. Whenever I put up a fight to free myself, Brian just became more aggressive. I couldn't bear to look him in the face. Instead I stared out the window at the streetlight. I could hear the sounds of Happy Birthday being sung downstairs to my Grandpa. While everyone else celebrated I lay in the dark being abused. Brian lay on top of me kissing my neck. He then started touching my chest and slowly made his way down the front of my pants. After touching and rubbing down my underwear Brian began inserting his finger inside me. I started to moan in pain and begged him to stop. Over and over I told him he was hurting me and the only thing he could say was I was tight. As tears streamed down my face I gripped the beanbag in pain. Brian ignored my tears and just told me to relax. When Brian was finished he told me to go get cake with him. That was the last thing I felt like eating, but if it would get me out of his room I would do anything. I went downstairs and grabbed the smallest piece of cake while Brian watched me. Brian sat at the same table in the kitchen with a grin on his face the entire time. In a way it felt like his way of celebrating the pain he was putting me through. We left soon after and now I am in bed and can't sleep. I don't know how I can go on living like this. I hurt so badly down there. When will I be free from Brian's power and control? Another night filled with tears.

Erin

JANUARY, 1998 2:40 A.M.

Dear God,

Please help me I can't take much more. I can barely sleep anymore. The nightmares have me tossing and turning in my sleep until I wake up and can't fall back asleep. I then start to imagine hearing things in my house or seeing shadows that really aren't there. This secret is killing me and I have to tell someone. What if Brian is right and no one believes me. How do I make him stop? If you are out there God please help me!

Erin

JANUARY, 1998 11:30 P.M.

Tonight Brian tried to abuse me at a family party for my cousin Megan. It began in the basement where Brian was trying to get me by the furnace, but I managed to make my way over to the washing machine and then escaped upstairs. Brian didn't follow but instead stayed downstairs with my sister Allie and my older cousins. Mom didn't come with us. It was just Allie, Dad and me. We nearly got in an accident on the way to my aunt and uncle's house. I was on edge all night, fully alert of my every step. I have school tomorrow so I better end this.

Erin

FEBRUARY, 1998 10:20 P.M.

I had a great birthday party. I turned thirteen and had a huge party at my house. On my actual birthday mom invited the family all over for dinner and cake. That was the last thing I wanted on my birthday. I was not looking forward to seeing Brian. When everyone arrived at seven I prayed just this one special day Brian would leave me alone. For dinner we had chicken potpie. After dinner I opened presents. I got clothes, games, purse, and a lot of money. From my Aunt Mary, Uncle Scott and the boys I received a writing board which comes in handy and refrigerator magnets. My Aunt Mary always has them on her fridge and knows I like them so she bought me a couple packages. I could use them on my locker next year in junior high. After opening my presents it was time for cake and ice cream. I already knew what my birthday wish was. It was the same wish every night I pray for. I wished that Brian would never hurt me again. I did my best to have fun on my birthday, but I was worried something would happen. Since I was getting so much attention from everyone, it didn't give Brian a chance to ever be alone with me. I can only pray it stays this way. With Allie's birthday coming up and then Caitlin's I will have to face Brian over and over again. Something I'm not looking forward to. For now though I'm going to get some sleep.

Erin

FEBRUARY, 1998 11:15 P.M.

My sister Caitlin is so mean. Tonight my Aunt Mary talked me into babysitting for her. Brian was out of town for the weekend so I knew I didn't have to worry. After I put David and Jake to bed, I was watching television in the family room. The phone rang and I answered it. On the other line was someone saying, "I'm watching you and I'm going to get you." Then the person hung up. I began to panic and was terrified it was Brian coming to get me. A few minutes later I received another call. This time the person on the other end told me they were watching my every move and hung up again. I decided to call my parents. My mom answered and I told her about the phone calls and how scared I was. Mom began telling my dad and then I heard laughter in the back round. Mom got back on the phone and said, "Erin don't worry it was Caitlin trying to scare you." I suddenly broke down and began crying to my mom on the phone. Over the phone I could hear mom yelling at Caitlin telling her how cruel of a prank she played and told her to apologize to me. Mom told me Caitlin is in trouble for this. If only mom knew the real horror I've been dealing with. Then she probably would understand why I reacted the way I did. I was so afraid it was Brian terrorizing me. I began crying because I was relieved it was only Caitlin. The rest of the night I kept hearing things like someone was watching me or breaking in the house. When my aunt came home I told her what Caitlin did and she agreed it was a cruel prank.

FEBRUARY, 1998 8:15 P.M.

It's been a week since my last entry and my prayers were shattered when Brian was preparing his next chance to use my body for his own pleasures. It happened yesterday when I went over to Brian's house because Aunt Mary invited Allie and me for dinner. Allie was upstairs playing with David and Jake while I made chocolate chip cookies with my aunt. The three of them kept calling me to come up and play with them. After putting the cookies in the oven I went upstairs. I saw that the boys and Allie were playing hide and go seek. I hadn't seen Brian all day so I joined in on hiding. I first hid in the bathroom upstairs. I was the first one to be found. So I counted the next round and found Allie first. I decided the next round to hide in my aunt and uncle's walk-in closet. It was dark so I crawled over to the corner and closed the door. I sat there silently and could hear Allie searching for us. Then totally unexpectedly I felt something grab my shoulder. I nearly wet my pants. I screamed, but Brian covered my mouth. I later learned he was in his room when I came upstairs and when I wasn't looking he walked into the closet and figured that would be a place to hide. My heart was pounding. Brian pulled me closer to him and then wrapped his legs around mine. Over and over I pleaded with him not to hurt me. With his legs wrapped around me Brian began forcing his hands down my pants and fondling me. His hands were so cold sending chills down my spine. Five minutes passed and we both heard Allie opening the closet door. She glanced in, but hanging clothes covered us and it was dark. When I saw her close the door and leave I just wanted to cry. Brian pulled his sweaty hands from my pants and began going up my shirt and slipping his hands under my training bra. Brian's deep breathing was hot against my ear sending chills down my back. Once again I was trapped under Brian's control in the dark. When it was all over, I had been in the closet for around twenty minutes. My plans were to walk home immediately, but that would make my aunt suspicious. I stuck around to have spaghetti, but dreaded every moment of it. Especially since anytime I eat anything with tomato sauce I feel like I am going to throw up reminding me of the first night I was abused and could taste the pizza in the back of my throat.

When dinner was over I thanked my aunt and proceeded to leave, but she stopped me and gave me a cookie I made. I grabbed the cookie from her and made my way to the back yard. Walking home I felt really dirty. Tears streamed down my face. It was at this point I decided to stop going to Brian's house, which meant I would have to do some lying. When I got home I turned on the bathtub and sat in tears asking God over and over to help me. That night as I lay in the dark I was imagining Brian's voice over and over again warning me if I told anyone no one would believe me and I would destroy our family. His strong words continue to keep me silent, but I'm not sure I can stay quiet much longer.

Erin

FEBRUARY, 1998 6:15 P.M.

Tonight my parents, Caitlin, and I went out to dinner for Caitlin's birthday. Allie had something going on and didn't come out with us. At dinner mom brought up the conversation of going on vacation. Well, mom brings that up all the time and it never happens. She talked about wanting to take us girls to Colorado. She said we would drive there because it is so beautiful, and I am terrified to fly. Mom said she would plan the whole trip. Caitlin and I both said we would believe it when we are there. Mom got us very excited though and right now in my life I am in need of a vacation. I stopped going over to Brian's house. The last time I was there was February ninth and today is the twenty fifth of February. I've been lying to my aunt. Every day she stops and asks me to watch the boys and I make up a new lie each time. I'm usually telling her I am going shopping, have a project to work on, or going to a friend's house. I hate lying to her though. I feel really guilty. Eventually after telling her "no" so many times, she began asking Allie to come over. I'm just glad to be away from Brian. I've been having terrible nightmares of being chased and raped. The nightmares keep me up at night. I almost told the school social worker about Brian, but I backed down from saying anything. I need some fresh air so I'm going to go take Chance for a walk.

Erin

FEBRUARY, 1998 10:15 P.M.

Emily and I made a time capsule and put different items from our childhood in it. We also wrote letters for the future. We then took it outside and buried it in the ground. I wonder how long it will be until we dig it up. I took my dog Chance on a long walk today. Actually he pulled me on roller blades. He is good at that. I love having a dog. I went past Brian's house while walking Chance and thankfully no one saw me. I wouldn't want my aunt stopping me. I'm starting to do better now that I'm staying away from Brian. Although I am lying to my aunt, I don't know what else to do. I am still having nightmares of Brian. At night I continue to leave my door open and closet light on. Tonight is no different. Good night!

Erin

MARCH, 1998 2:35 A.M.

I just want to die. I am in so much pain and can't stop crying. It got really bad tonight. I feel so dirty right now. I'm sitting in bed with images running through my head of tonight. Around five tonight my Aunt Mary called at the last minute asking if I could baby-sit. She was desperate because her other babysitter blew her off at the last minute and she had plans to go to Chicago with Uncle Scott. Before saying "yes" I asked where the older boys would be and she explained they had hockey and both were spending the night at a friend's house. I thought about it and knew my mom's birthday is next month and could use some money to buy her something. I could also hear how desperate my aunt was. I told her I would see her in a half hour. When I got over there my aunt and uncle were in a rush and I only saw them for a few moments before they left handing me their cell number and telling me they would be home around one or one-thirty. I spent the night playing with the boys. I chased them around the house, played board games with them, and hide and go seek, and then I let them play a little Nintendo. For dinner I made them macaroni and cheese, which is the only thing I really know how to make other then sandwiches and throwing a pizza in the oven. I let them both have some ice cream before putting them to bed at nine. I read Jake a couple books and then turned on his night-light. I went in my aunt and uncle's bedroom to watch TV. I turned on channel five to see that Dateline was on. I began watching it. It was a story about a mom dying of cancer and making home videos for her young daughter to watch when she got older. It was so sad, but so thoughtful of this mom. While watching the show I heard a noise from downstairs. I ignored it and continued to watch the show. A few minutes later I heard it again. I started to get a little nervous, but knew it was just the house making noises, but when you are alone your imagination starts to go. So I did my best to ignore the noise. Another five minutes passed when once again I heard the noise a lot closer, but this time didn't stop to think about it until it was too late. I heard the door of my aunt and uncle's bedroom closing and standing there was Brian locking the door. I immediately jumped to the other side of the bed and asked in a panicked voice why he was home. He told me his game was cancelled so he just decided to come home since it was still early. I knew he was lying and the truth was he knew I was here by myself. I tried telling Brian about the show I was watching, but he wasn't interested. Brian started to make his way towards me so I climbed on the bed to unlock the door and leave. Just as I was about to get off the bed, Brian grabbed my ankle. I told him to let go and he insisted that I play with him. I told him I needed to check on the boys. The struggle began and I knew I had to win this one because my aunt and uncle weren't going to be home for hours and I couldn't endure the pain he was going to put me through for that long. I struggled on the bed with Brian as he tried to gain control of me. The entire time he laughed. Brian finally was sitting on top of me and I did the only thing in my power to do. With one hand free I punched him in the balls. He fell off me and I was able to run to the door and unlock it. I ran down stairs in a panic and paced back and forth in the kitchen not knowing what to do. I listened to hear if Brian was coming downstairs. Five minutes after I punched him I could hear the sound of Brian's footsteps making his way down the stairs. I felt as if I was watching a horror movie. The only difference is I was in the movie. I stood in the kitchen until Brian appeared and we began playing a game of cat and mouse running around in circles trying to escape him. Then he stopped and I didn't know where he went so I decided to make a mad dash for the upstairs and was going to wake the boys. I could hear Brian behind me chasing me up the stairs. Just when I was about to open the door I felt Brian's hand on my shoulder telling me to step away. I opened the door and Brian told me to let them sleep. Grabbing my wrist Brian began pulling me telling me to come back in his parents' bedroom. With nowhere to turn I fought and fought and started to grow weak. As we grew closer to his parents' room I begged him not to have sex with me. Back in his parents' room I jumped on the bed crawling to the other side. Brian locked the door and said he wanted to talk to me. I knew that was nothing but a bunch of crap. The struggle began again until Brian was on top of me once more. I wasn't ready to give up, but the more I struggled the more Brian hurt me. Like usual the way to control me was pinching my butt every time I fought back. I looked in his eyes and saw a look of evil. Slowly I grew weak and could no longer fight back. My body lay motionless as Brian began touching me. The lights were on for once so I could see everything around me. I stare at the clock reading nine-thirty-eight p.m. Every minute felt like an hour. The television still played in the background as Brian lay on top of me with his dark green shirt against my face. I could feel his heart beating rapidly against my chest. His heavy breathing echoed through my ears. His warm lips bracing my neck and his hands grasping my hair sent chills down my back. Holding back the tears I closed my eyes as Brian began unzipping my jean pants and pulling them down around my thighs. I went away in my head trying to imagine myself somewhere else. I imagined myself on a warm beach with the sun. Trying to pretend to hear the sounds of waves instead of Brian's heavy breathing. The pain was too extreme as Brian forced his finger inside me. I couldn't take much more and felt paralyzed with fear. I prayed every time I heard a car pass outside that it would be my aunt and uncle. My hopes would rise until I would hear the cars pass the house. The abuse continued for the next two hours, two of the longest hours in my entire life. I just wanted to block it all out, but the pain was too extreme. At one point he grabbed my hand and tried forcing me to hold his penis. I made a tight fist and refused as he pulled my hand down his pants and up against it. He must have placed his hands on every part of my body. The chills he would send up and down my spine. The noises he would make when forcing his finger inside me. Noises I never want to hear again. He said very little the entire night. As he became more physical I prayed he would not rape me. Just when I was about to give up all hope, I heard another car coming down the street, but this one slowed down. I looked over at the clock that read five minutes after midnight. I knew it couldn't be my aunt and uncle who said they'd be home around one. It wasn't until I heard the sound of the garage door opening that I felt a sense of relief. Brian immediately jumped to his feet and went to unlock the door. Before heading down the hallway, he looked at me laying on the bed and reminded me that this was our secret and if I were to tell no one would believe me and I would be at fault. When I got downstairs I met my aunt in the kitchen who asked how the night went. If only she knew what really went on the past two hours. I almost broke down and cried in front of her. The two-minute drive to my house I sat in silence. My aunt told me I looked really tired when she pulled up in my driveway. She handed me an extra ten dollars for coming on such short notice. I felt like shoving the ten dollars back at her and telling her what a sick evil son she has, but instead I smiled and she watched me walk in the house. The house was dark so I quietly went up to the bathroom and placed a hot washrag on my face and began sobbing and shaking. I sat rocking myself back and forth and could still feel Brian's hands all over my chest, and down my pants. Looking in the mirror, I saw that my eyes were bloodshot and my face was very red. I considered climbing in the bathtub to scrub away the dirty feelings I felt, but afraid that it would wake my parents. I now lay in bed as I soak my pillow with my tears. I don't want to wake to see tomorrow.

Erin

MARCH 1998 8:05 P.M.

I'm in Wisconsin as I write this. I've been hurting inside. The feelings of Brian are all over me. Mom has been very concerned about me. She keeps asking me if everything is all right. She has noticed a huge difference in my mood. She asked me this morning if I am sad about something. If only I could tell her the truth. Instead I look her in the face and tell her everything is fine.

Today my mom and dad set up the trampoline. It was fun jumping on it. Next week is spring break. My Aunt Mary called for me to baby-sit and I told her I was busy and couldn't. I was working on my autobiography for school. It is a huge three-hundred-point assignment of our entire lives. The first two chapters are non-fiction. The rest we have to make up. After I told my aunt I couldn't baby-sit she told me she was coming over and I began to panic. My mom told me to chill and to just let my aunt know that I was working on a homework assignment. My mom couldn't understand why I was making such a big issue out of it. If mom knew the terrible truth of the past two years she'd understand. My aunt came in and talked with my mom, I showed her my autobiography. I refused to baby sit for my aunt who left shortly after visiting. At night I toss and turn in my sleep and see Brian's face in every dream. I just want someone to take this pain away. Well I am about to watch a movie with the family. I'll write more during spring break.

Erin

MARCH, 1998 9:45 P.M.

I'm sitting in my bedroom in tears. I learned something today that has me very upset. I feel so much guilt and shame. It all began this weekend when Allie and I brought Emily up to Wisconsin. The weekend was going great. We spent most the weekend at the beach or on the trampoline. Today while walking back from the beach Allie turned to Emily and me and said, "Brian's gross." I got a lump in my throat and didn't want to believe what Allie just said. For a moment it felt like everything froze in time and Allie's words echoed through my head. Emily and I immediately looked at each other in shock. We both knew what Allie meant. I went on to ask Allie if Brian had been touching her. Allie looked surprised to hear me asking her and then told us that it was true. By the time we got to our house we all went over to the trampoline and talked. Mom and dad weren't home. As we sat on the trampoline I told Allie that Brian had been touching me for two-years. Allie told us that it only happened three times to her. Together Allie and I knew it was time to go to mom. While sitting on the trampoline I explained to Allie that after we come out about the abuse our lives will never be the same. I told her if the rest of the family found out they might not believe us. Allie went on to tell me what Brian did to her. I learned that he abused her the same Thanksgiving that he did me. He also abused her that night in the basement down by the furnace the same time he tried doing it to me. Right after I went upstairs he went for Allie. Right now I have so much guilt. If only I had told the first time it happened in the condo, Allie wouldn't have to go through this. It is my entire fault. Mom is downstairs right now looking at different music. She was just hired to sing in restaurants and is very excited. By telling her about Brian I will take away her excitement. I told Allie to wait until tomorrow before we told mom. There is no way I'll be sleeping tonight. After tonight my secret will be exposed and I won't be so alone. I'll write tomorrow after we tell mom. All I can do is pray that everything goes ok.

Erin

MARCH, 1998 1:45 A.M.

It is late here, almost two in the morning. It has been a very long day. My day started off by going to my friend Melissa's house. We decided to go shopping for the day. While I was at her house Allie was at her best friend's house. We took our bikes to my house and on the way there I asked Melissa if she had any secrets she kept from her parents. She didn't really know what I was trying to get at so I told her I had a secret my parents didn't know about. The whole way home she tried getting it out of me. When we got to my house I saw Allie and her friend Kathleen sitting in the sunroom with my mom. I could tell by the look on all three of their faces that my mom had just been told something that shocked her. It was a look of anger and disgust. My mom began talking to my friend Melissa about good summer books to read. I told mom that we were riding our bikes to the store to go shopping. Mom told me she had to show me something in my room before we left. I knew right then she knew the truth. While walking up the stairs I looked back at Allie and Kathleen and the look on Allie's face gave it away. When mom walked in her room and closed the door she told me to sit on the bed. I sat down and mom looked up at me and said," I know what Brian's been doing to you. You're safe now and he will never hurt you again." She gave me a big hug and tears began to form in her eyes. A huge sense of relief came over me. I no longer had to live in silence. She told me we would discuss it tonight when dad got home. I could see the tears falling from my mom's eyes as she watched me walk out of her room. I met Melissa at the bottom of the stairs were the two of us went outside and got on our bikes. The whole way to the store I told Melissa what Brian and done. She was in shock. When I got home later I walked in to see my mom, Caitlin, and Allie all sitting in the kitchen. Caitlin was in disbelief and couldn't imagine Brian doing something like this. When dad finally came home he gave me a big hug and told me I don't ever have to keep a secret like this from him. Mom and dad had talked and decided dad was going to walk over to Aunt Mary's to talk to her. I walked over tonight with dad. My other uncle lives next door so I sat on his deck while my dad went to the front door. I could hear my dad asking if it was a bad time to talk. I sat there on the deck looking over at Brian's house knowing he was somewhere in there not knowing I just broke my silence. I then looked up in the sky at the stars. I began praying to God to make everything go ok and to comfort me. When dad finally came around the corner I got up and walked down the path back to our house. My dad told my Aunt Mary. She was in shock and said she would talk to Brian with Uncle Scott. For the first time in two years I am not going to bed with a terrible secret that is eating away inside me. I'm no longer alone. I can rest tonight knowing Brian will never hurt me again. Good night.

Erin

APRIL, 1998 9:40 P.M.

I knew it! Brian is not admitting to the truth. I hate him so much. My mom talked to aunt Mary. Aunt Mary said that Uncle Scott and she talked to Brian and he told them that Allie and me were making it up. He always told me he would not confess to it, but it just makes me so mad that he is going to try saying he didn't do any of this. My anger is boiling. My Aunt and Uncle believe Brian and aren't going to do anything about it, which has my mom furious. My mom has been trying to call my aunt all week, but no one will answer and we know they are home. My mom is planning on going to the police next.

Erin

APRIL, 1998 10:45 P.M.

I had a terrible Easter. It was the first time I was seeing Brian since I broke my silence. I was so scared! While flying kites I walked past him in the grass field. Brian looked at me and gave me a dirty glare. A glare I'll never forget. Brian is still lying and my parents are having a meeting with Brian's parents about the whole situation. My mom is putting Allie and I in counseling. Our first appointment is this Thursday at three. I don't know if I am ready to talk about any of this. I just wanted it all to end and go away. My Aunt Mary wanted to keep everything between my parents and her, but behind our backs she told everyone in the family and made very light of the situation, which really upsets me. She has no right to say anything because she doesn't even know any details. I've never seen my mom so hurt and angry before. Well, I will write more tomorrow. This is just the beginning of a long road ahead.

Erin

APRIL, 1998 5:00 P.M.

I went to the family-counseling center today. My parents, Caitlin, Allie and I all went. Our counselor's name is Judy.

Judy asked a bunch of questions, which was difficult, but I managed. We set up appointments to see her every Thursday at four. Judy felt it best if I saw her by myself to see if I could start talking about the abuse. I would much rather not talk about it at all, but I know that it is unhealthy. On top of dealing with all this I am also having eye surgery in June. I am scared about that. Dad just walked in my room to see how I've been doing. Both my parents have been very supportive. Well, Chance needs to be walked. I no longer walk down the path towards Brian's house. It is like I freeze up and can't move forward so I always turn around before I get there. Mom and Dad have a second meeting with Brian's parents tonight. Mom tells me Aunt Mary doesn't want to believe Allie and me. The truth will eventually come out.

Erin

APRIL, 1998 12:05 A.M.

Mom was downstairs crying on the phone tonight to her friend. I overheard her saying, "I should have seen the warning signs, and they were all there for me to see." Mom has been crying a lot. Brian is still not confessing so I took action tonight and picked up the phone and called his house. Brian happened to answer and I told him not to hang up. I was shaking and I am sure Brian could hear the quiver in my voice. I asked him why he was calling Allie and me liars. I then told Brian my mom is calling the police tomorrow morning and making a report. I then heard Brian telling his parents. Brian got back on the phone and asked if he and his parents could come over and discuss this. I told him I would call him back. Brian was the last person I wanted to see. I went downstairs and told my mom about my conversation with Brian. Mom totally disagreed with having him come over and said that would be secondary abuse to Allie and me. Uncle Scott called around eleven and left a message saying "I" wanted the meeting. I never wanted anything! There he goes again lying. My parent didn't pick it up and let the machine get the rest of it. Well, it is late and I have school tomorrow. Good night

Erin

APRIL, 1998 9:45 P.M.

Today I went to medieval times with my sixth-grade class. It was fun being with all my friends. Mom went to the police station and made a police report on Brian this morning. Mom has made many phone calls trying to figure out how to handle it. After school today mom sat down with Allie and me and told us that we will be going to this place called, "The Children's Advocacy Center." It is a place where kids who have been abused go and get interviewed. Mom said it is normal to feel afraid, but not to worry as there are good people there. We are being interviewed next week at the center. The same day we leave for Colorado, April 30th. Our appointment is in the morning so mom is pulling us out of school for the whole day because we will leave for Colorado at noon, anyway. My teacher, Mrs. Miller, stopped me after school to see how I was doing. She told me she was concerned because I haven't been very happy. I told her a little of what was going on at home and she was very sorry and said if I needed to talk she was there for me. I just want things to get back to normal. I just want to be a normal kid with no worries. I'm very tired. Good night!

Erin

APRIL, 1998 5:30 P.M.

I saw my counselor Judy today. I talked about the interview mom was telling me about. Judy asked how I felt about it and I told her I was nervous. We also talked about my upcoming eye surgery and how scared I am about it. Judy taught me a relaxation technique to help reduce my fears and anxiety. I thought it was a crazy idea when she had me closing my eyes and imagine little holes in my feet, but when I continued to listen I actually started to feel a little at ease. Judy said we would practice it again so when I would go in for surgery I could use it. I guess the reason why I am so scared about the surgery is because I am going to have no control. Brian abused me in my sleep. Having surgery they have to put you to sleep and I don't like not being in control. Judy wished me good luck with my interview and told me to have fun in Colorado. All I have to remember is to take some deep breaths. The big day is two days away. I'm safe now and that is what I must keep reminding myself. I have so much going on in my life from breaking my silence to my upcoming eye surgery. It is too much for one kid to handle. What happened to the good days? When I knew no pain. Well, it is time for dinner. Night!

Erin

APRIL, 1998 8:15 A.M.

We are leaving in an hour to go to the center to be interviewed. After that it is off to Colorado. I am really nervous. I haven't told anyone the details of what Brian put me through. I hope I will be able to open up. I'm really scared right now. I have to remember to breathe. I'll write again when we are on the road to Colorado.

Erin

APRIL, 1998 11:45 A.M.

We are just pulling out of the Children's Advocacy Center and I made it through the morning. When we arrived a lady who is called an advocate greeted us. The advocate, Larissa, explained her role in our case. Larissa then asked us if we wanted juice boxes and bagels. About ten minutes later she came out with a warm bagel with cream cheese and juice for Allie and me and coffee for mom. The waiting room had two big couches and tons of toys. There was a TV and VCR, which had plenty of movies to choose from. Allie and I put a movie in and sat at a round table and colored. Larissa took my mom into a room to talk and closed the door. What they were talking about I have no idea. It seemed like forever before mom finally came out. Larissa pointed out all the stuffed animals on the floor and informed Allie and I that we could take one home after our interview. As Allie and me sat there pointing out the cute stuffed animals, another lady appeared and entered them room. She introduced herself as Megan. She said she was a social worker. Larissa told us we would be going to a room with her to talk. Since I am the older sister, she asked if I'd go first. While Allie and mom stayed in the waiting room,

I got up and followed the social worker. I passed a bunch of stuffed animals along the ground. I went down a hallway and was led into a small room. I immediately noticed a huge mirror in the room. I don't understand why a mirror that size would be in a room that tiny. In the room was a round table and chairs and in the corner there were beanbags. The room was very colorful. I sat down at the table and noticed the two naked dolls under the table. The social worker began asking me questions. She started by asking me if I knew the difference between the truth and a lie. I told her a lie is when someone is saying something that isn't true or made up. Megan then started to ask about my family life. About five minutes into our conversation she asked me about my cousin Brian. She then asked if I could talk about my cousin Brian with her. I took a deep breath and kept staring at myself in the large mirror. After describing different incidents where Brian took advantage of me, the social worker pulled out the two naked dolls from under the table.

I had to look away at the mirror until I could get a hold of myself. Megan kept reminding me to take my time. They never told me I was going to have to show what Brian did to me. I sat staring at the two naked dolls as images of Brian abusing me began playing over in my head. I started to show Megan with the dolls exactly what Brian did. It got harder and harder telling story after story that I tried forgetting over the past two years of the abuse. It was very difficult and I was holding back the tears. With Megan's support and encouragement I got through the interview. Although I told a lot of detail, I didn't get into how bad the abuse got. It was too painful and fresh to talk about. Megan gave me a pat on the back and told me I did wonderfully. She walked me back to my mom and Allie. Allie was still coloring, but stopped and asked me how it was before following Megan back to the room. While Allie was gone mom asked how I did. I told her I was nervous and scared, but made it through.

After the interview I felt a sense of relief. It was like ten pounds had been lifted off my shoulders. For once I didn't feel so alone and lost in the world. I now knew I had people who cared. When Allie eventually returned and Larissa came back to the waiting room and asked for mom, Larissa and mom walked away and headed for the upstairs. Allie and I played a board game called "Candy Land" while we waited. A while later mom returned and Larissa told us we did a great job today and pointed to all the stuffed animals and told us to go pick one out. She then wished us a good time in Colorado. When we got back outside the sky was blue and the sun was shinning. I took in some fresh air and was in need of this vacation. When we were pulling out of the parking lot I looked back and made a promise to myself that one day I would return to the center and show my appreciation for what they did for my family and me. I no longer feel I am alone in this scary world. We just picked up my sister Caitlin at the high school and now we are on the road to Colorado. I'll write more when we get home from Colorado. I have a sixteen-hour road trip ahead of me.

Erin

MAY, 1998 8:30 P.M.

We had an awesome time in Colorado. We hiked in the mountains and passed so much wildlife. Listening to the river and the different wildlife roaming around was a soothing feeling. It brought me a sense of peace. We saw deer and elk throughout the whole trip. We also went into towns and shopped. I didn't want to leave, but had no other choice. It was good to see my dog Chance when we got back. When we got home there was a message on the machine for my mom from the detective at the police station. I later learned that the police called Brian in with his parents. The police talked to his parents first and then asked to speak to Brian alone. While speaking to Brian the detective got Brian to confess to abusing Allie and me. It was a sense of relief to know he confessed. Since my parents did not want to bring this to court and drag Allie and I through the ordeal of a trial, we agreed on having Brian get sex offender counseling, probation, and having him not be able to come within one hundred feet of Allie and me without an adult present. I just can't get over the fact that he confessed. He also has to do community service. I never thought I would see the day when Brian would confess. Well, I am glad it ended the way it did. Brian must have been feeling guilty.

Erin

MAY, 1998 6:45 P.M.

I saw Judy today. I told her about Brian confessing and she was surprised. She asked how it made me feel and I told her I was relieved, but also scared. My teacher sent home a letter today and told me to give it to my mom. When I got home mom opened it and the letter was about having me talk to the district social worker. My teacher was concerned about me. Mom called her after reading it and explained that I was already getting help, but thanked her for caring.

I am getting excited for camp. Emily and I will be leaving in a week with a bunch of other students and two teachers. It is energy encounter camp that is held in Wisconsin. I am in need of these vacations. It is keeping me busy and keeping my mind off other things. I also learned this week that, when I was interviewed and couldn't understand why there was a huge mirror in the room, I was being watched through my entire interview by a detective. I am so glad I didn't know that when I went into the interview, but thinking back now during my interview I stared at the mirror most of the time thinking I was looking at myself when really I was looking at people behind the two-way mirror. Anyway I must end this here. I'm just glad it is done with.

Erin

MAY, 1998 7:30 P.M.

My dad got really angry today. My dad never gets angry. He was over at my grandpa's house and my grandpa turned to my dad and began talking about Brian. Grandpa told my dad he couldn't see Brian ever doing anything to Allie or me. That is all dad needed to hear and he lost it. He told my grandpa that he had no right to say that and Allie and Erin are telling the truth. From the sounds of it my dad was very upset. He really hasn't shown his emotions around me. I don't think he wants me to see him angry and upset, which is probably the best thing for me.

Erin

MAY, 1998 5:30 P.M.

I'm at camp right now in Wisconsin. I am in the cabin with Kathleen and Emily. It looks like we have a fun week ahead of us. I feel bad for Allie. She wanted to come. We have to cook our own food every day over a campfire. I'm going to take lots of pictures. It should be an interesting experience. I'll write more when I get home.

MAY, 1998 1:30 P.M.

Mom and Dad along with my sisters picked me up at the school after coming back from camp. We decided to go to McDonalds for breakfast. I could tell the whole ride home something wasn't right. It was almost like something happened while I was away. Mom seemed upset and everyone else seemed quiet. I started to question my parents when finally my mom informed me that one of my uncles sent her a very unpleasant e-mail during the week. When we got home mom showed me the e-mail along with her response. This is what the letter said.

Bekki,

Don't take this as being friendly. Personally, and this is my opinion only, not anyone else's, you should have stayed in Colorado. The crap you pulled with Mary and Scott stinks and considering that your daughter said something was supposed to have happened here at my home has me very upset. You know damn well, or you would have bothered to check your story first, that your kids were never alone in my home. Someone over the age of sixteen was with them at all times. The fact that you called the Schaumburg police and then left town stinks. The call to DCFS was totally unnecessary. If something had happened anywhere, you should have talked to the parents first. The extremely ill feelings that you have caused a lot of us are feelings towards you and Dan and your kids, is your fault and no one else's. Maybe you could explain to all of us why you refused to see the counselor with Mary and Scott? You brought this all on yourself. For the record . . . you and the kids are not welcome in my home. If you were invited here it would not be at my wish, but others in the family whom I respect.

Mike

Mike,

I wasn't going to respond to your last E-mail. . . . because anyone who would write anything so mean and twisted . . . well just being you has to be miserable enough! I don't think you realize how transparent your e-mail was on your own issues . . . to have taken it so personally . . . makes me wonder if you must have a few skeletons rattling in your closet! I hope you end up dealing with them . . . I'll keep you in my prayers. As far as the facts in your e-mail go . . . well, if you choose to be ignorant that is your choice . . . I feel really bad for Mary and Scott too, but you have your victims mixed up. Brian is the one who hurt my girls, us and Mary and Scott. Mary is in so much pain she needs to vent her anger at someone and it's hard to do it when it's your own son. Mike if you want to be fair you would have asked our side not assumed and spewed! Mary did not want to work with us. She would not return our phone calls and believed her son was innocent. (And I don't blame her that would be hard). Dan and I sought the advice of not one, but ten counselors, including children advocacy, social workers, and a detective on how we could handle this without reporting it. We did everything in our power and the end result being he denied it and Mary and Scott were going to let it be. They were advised to have a family meeting with the girls present and Dan and I felt that was secondary abuse to our girls and unheard of (if you even care to know). So Dan and I took action to get Brian the help he needed through professionals. The detective told me Mary and Scott felt Brian was innocent and obviously they didn't tell you, Mike, that Brian confessed to all the abuse while being interviewed by a detective . . . including that incident in your house. The sixteen year olds must have turned their heads!

Mike, there are over thirteen different accounts of abuse to Allie and Erin that we know of. They are in counseling with Dan and me. It pisses me off, and makes me wonder about you and your opinion when little girls get sexually abused and you call them liars, and me a jerk for protecting them and giving them the message that they matter. If Brian had stolen a radio from Kmart it would have been a police matter. You obviously think my girls' innocence, bodies, and minds are worth less than that. I feel sorry for you. If an adult woman is sexually assaulted it is a police matter. Who the hell do you think is supposed to take care of young girls? Yes, their parents. Brian confessed, he will now get help and than he can be restored. Now isn't that better than denying it and holding it in his whole life. For the record no one else in the family who Dan and I care about are blaming us. So your little threat has no bearing! As far as me getting help, I did, Mike, and that is why my girls were taken care of when someone hurt them! Statistic shows most child abuse happens within family and that is why it continues. I hope you were just confused, Mike, because if you weren't I'll be praying for you.

Bekki

I am in shock that my own uncle could be so mean. It hurts so bad to hear him write this. My mom called my grandma and read her the letter my uncle sent and it upset my grandma. She told my mom she'd be calling him. My grandparents are in denial about the abuse too. Our entire family is in denial except for my parents. The rest of the family wants the truth to disappear. They are brushing it off like it was no big deal. It angers me just thinking about it.

Erin

JUNE, 1998 10:45 P.M.

My surgery is this Tuesday, June 9th. That is two days away and I am terrified. I hate being put to sleep. I have so much anxiety that something is going to go wrong. I couldn't even get excited for the last day of school because I was too nervous knowing I had this operation coming up. I am no longer at Blackwell Elementary School. I will be attending Jane Addams Junior High in September. It will be a whole new experience for me. The last week of school was spent celebrating. All the sixth graders had a party in the gym where we played games and ate food. We took class photos, too. It is going to be a big adjustment from going to a small school to a much larger school. I will be switching teachers every hour. Well, I must get some sleep. Good night.

Erin

JUNE, 1998 9:15 P.M.

It has been almost a week since I had my operation. When I woke up I was in so much pain. I felt like I had been beaten up. My eyes were swollen and I was very tired. Something I never want to go through again but I have another operation coming up again in August. In that operation they are putting tiny tubes in my eyes. In that operation I just had was on one eye. They cut open the eyelid and raised it. As you can see, my eyes are a mess. This has not been the year for me. I am not seeing Judy anymore. I just don't want to talk about the past at all. I don't know how to open up and talk about my feelings. It is all so hard for me. There is so much I haven't told anyone yet. I never got into detail during my interview about how bad the abuse got. I left a lot of detail out about that last night Brian abused me. The night he was very forceful with me. I see my mom crying a lot at night to my dad or on the phone with her friends. This whole thing has been very hard for her and I don't want her to see me struggling. I want to show her that I am strong. She is having a hard enough time dealing with this all. She doesn't need to see me hurting. I do my best to keep myself busy, but deep down I am holding in pain. I am going to camp again in July with my cousins and sisters in Michigan. It should be fun. Well, I don't plan on writing much this summer. So I will write again towards the end of summer. Good night!

AUGUST, 1998 10:05 P.M.

I had an awesome time at camp. I stayed in a cabin and made a bunch of new friends. I got up every morning and did polar bear. Polar bear is where you get up before seven and walk down to the beach and jump in the water. It is a big wake up call. The food is excellent here. They make the best French toast. During the day my cabin has a schedule and every day is different. Some days we go canoeing, to art room, archery, swimming, dodge ball, and we had a dance one night. Every day we have an hour of time to ourselves in our cabins where we must stay. People sleep, write letters home, read, or quietly talk to friends. After dinner at night everyone joins hands and we walk to the campfire together. At the campfire we sing songs. My favorite song we sing is "Angels Watching Over Me." From the campfire we go get ready for bed and lights are out at ten. Then the party begins. We all get in trouble because we are supposed to go to bed instead of giggling and walking around. You'll hear people outside cabin row shouting out different cabin numbers and telling them to go to bed.

On the last day of camp I cried. I made so many new friends and didn't want to say good-bye. I got addresses and promised to write them all. Going to camp was my best experience all summer.

Erin

SEPTEMBER, 1998 7:30 P.M.

The first day of junior high is tomorrow and I am really nervous. Emily's brother is coming over and walking to the bus stop with me. Allie and Emily are sixth graders at Blackwell. This is the first year I won't be in the same school as them. I am looking forward to a change in schools though. I like new things.

I had another operation. It was a lot worse than the first operation. I woke up and both my eyes were swollen. I could barely open them. There were tiny tubes in my eyes. When I got home Allie and Emily had called a bunch of people the night before and invited them over to my house for a surprise get-well party. I wasn't in the mood to have fun, but really wanted to. The anesthesia still hadn't worn off completely. I thanked them all for coming, but they didn't stay long after I came home. They all brought presents and balloons for me, which I thought was nice and didn't feel they had to do that for me.

I got my haircut and highlighted today. I want to go to school with a new look. I hope I like all my teachers. I have to go brush my teeth and get ready for bed. Good night!

Erin

SEPTEMBER, 1998 10:00 P.M.

It has been a good school year so far. Junior high is tough, but I like most of my teachers. My math teacher doesn't know how to teach. She hands out papers and expects you to know what you are doing. She is on an oxygen tank and will be having surgery soon so we will have a sub the rest of the year. I really like my science teacher. His name is Mr. Graba and going to his class is always a good laugh. I am not the best at science either, but I really like his teaching style. I am taking Spanish, but I don't know how that is going to be. It is hard for me. I am also in chorus, which will be a lot of fun. I must get some sleep. Oh, I almost forgot we got a kitten this month. Allie and I found her in a barn up the street. She was abandoned in a chicken coop. So we named her Chicken. Dad said we couldn't keep her, but mom said if we could get her home without dad seeing then we could. I had the kitten under my sweatshirt the whole way home. Allie and I had to sing so dad wouldn't hear the kitten cry.

Good night!

Erin

OCTOBER, 1998 9:00 P.M.

This weekend as we were leaving for Wisconsin I put on winter coat from last year and found a bunch of pictures in the front pocket. I started looking through them and came across one of Brian in his football jersey. Mom was standing outside with me and I showed her and she took it from me.

She reached into her pocket and pulled out her lighter, then she lit the picture on fire and we both watched it burn. In a way it felt good.

Erin

NOVEMBER, 1998 9:30 P.M.

I am babysitting for two-month-old triplets with Emily. We go over every day and help out a mother near our home. She had three boys. They are adorable little babies. Tomorrow I go into surgery to take the tubes out that have been in my eyes since this summer. I am nervous even though I have been put to sleep two times now. I still worry about it. At the end of the month I will have my last operation, but for that one I will be awake. It is laser surgery. As far as new friends go I met a lot of new people at school. Ali and Laura are my two new friends and Kassie is my new best friend. Laura spent the night this weekend. We had a lot of fun. I scared her too. I was invited to a Halloween party with a bunch of girls from my school and I scared everyone with my grandma costume. I have been a grandma every Halloween since I was in first grade and got the act down perfect. I use a cane and everything. Well, it is getting late and I have to be at the hospital at six-thirty in the morning so I better go to sleep.

Erin

NOVEMBER, 1998 8:30 P.M.

My surgery went well. I actually felt good afterwards unlike other surgeries. I'm going in Friday for laser surgery. I have been feeling really depressed lately. I've been having these memories of my abuse reappear and it is taking its toll on me. Then at night I have horrible nightmares of being attacked. I am just really struggling, but trying not to show it. School has been tough, too. I just have too much going on in my life for me. I dread the holidays, but thankfully we are spending Thanksgiving at our house with my cousins from

Michigan who are coming which will be nice. I won't have to see Brian. Every time I see him I get chills. Mom had a talk with me and knows I am holding a lot in. She has been really worried. She called the Children's Advocacy Center and they have a group for girls who have been sexually abused. It starts next month and mom asked if I was interested. I told her I would give it a try, but don't know if I am ready to really talk about any of this. I do feel it will be nice to be around other girls that can relate to me. I feel so alone dealing with everything. I thought when the abuse stopped I could move on with my life. Instead I am still running from Brian. The only difference is now I am running from him in my dreams. Well, I have to get ready for bed.

Erin

NOVEMBER, 1998 9:30 P.M.

The nightmares I've been having are horrible. I can't escape this nightmare hell I face every night. It is terrifying and I wake up in a panic. In every dream Brian is hurting me. At night I am afraid to go to sleep. I keep my door open and my closet light on. I also leave my television on, but dad turns it off before he goes to bed. I don't know what to do to move on.

Erin

DECEMBER, 1998 10:05 P.M.

I'm starting group soon and I hope it will help me. Maybe I'll learn how to deal with these memories. I went to the mall yesterday with Emily. We had so much fun. I don't think I ever laughed so hard before. We were having too much fun. Well, I am not looking forward to Christmas. I will have to see Brian Christmas Eve and day, which sucks. I am going Christmas shopping tomorrow with two of my friends. This is all for now.

Erin

DECEMBER, 1998 4:15 PM.

My mom called the sex offender program today to check on how everything was going with Brian. The person she talked to said they don't have any records for Brian and told my mom to call the States Attorney. My mom made a call to them and learned some very upsetting information. I guess my Aunt Mary fought for Brian so he wouldn't have a record. She wanted to send him to her own counselor because, if he went through the sex offender program, he would have a record and not be able to play football at the high school. The States Attorney told my mom that my aunt was the biggest bitch they ever had to deal with. The State Attorney eventually gave my aunt the ok, but wanted papers to show that Brian was getting help. What the state attorney didn't know is we only charged Brian with three charges. She did not know how much abuse he did and after talking to my mother was devastated. She told my mom that the therapist they made Brian see was for short term, meaning only two or three sessions. And the therapist sent a letter to the states attorney stating that Brian takes full responsibility for his actions and isn't a threat to society for his minor actions. I am so angry right now. How could you call his actions Minor? The hell he put me through was major. My parents are outraged, especially my mom. It just isn't fair. Our justice system fails once again. I have to end this entry here or else I get worked up in all this. I am just really upset and don't know what to do with all my feelings.

Erin

DECEMBER, 1998 10:45 P.M.

I went to group today. Today was mainly a get-to-know-you kind of day. The lady in charge of our group is Cathy. She is a therapist and works for the center. The girls in the group were all around the same age as me. There was Ashley, Jenny, Carey, Laura, Lindsey, and Jessica. There were also another girl named Kelly, but she couldn't make the first group. We did a lot of activities. We did a wall climb outside, played a maze game, and another game where we had to play in a circle. There were donuts and juice when we got there and for lunch we had pizza. I think I am really going to like being in a group like this. I think it might really help me. Our next group isn't until January because of the holidays. It gives me something to look forward to. Good night!

Erin

Denial

*"You cannot change the truth,
but the truth can change you."*

—Unknown

March, 1999 10:00 p.m.

We did an activity tonight in group where we all laid down on the carpet in the dark and had to close our eyes. Cathy told us a relaxation story about being on an island. We had to imagine we were on this island and only good things were on this island. We could put anything we wanted on it and it was suppose to represent something safe to us. She told us to use this exercise whenever we are feeling unsafe or scared. It was a neat exercise. We talked about suicide tonight and I admitted to having thoughts about it. Cathy was very supportive and understands. She informed all of us if we are ever in a situation where we feel suicidal to call her or go to someone immediately. Cathy became concerned and after group she talked to mom and feels it best if I see her one on one. So next week I will be doing that.

Erin

MARCH, 1999 9:40 P.M.

I saw Cathy today. We talked one on one in one of the inter-viewing rooms. I haven't been back in the interview room since my own interview almost a year ago. She really is trying to get me to let go of holding on to all my pain. Bottling it up isn't doing me any good. It is just too painful to talk about and I was hoping it would just go away after I came out about the abuse. Cathy told me I have a lot of strength and it is all right to let go of my pain. I am going to work a little each week to talk about things. We are splitting up our group and putting some of the younger girls in their own group and we are get-ting a few people added to ours. Kelly from my group had a sleep over at my house Saturday night. Sunday we went to the movies and saw a great movie called "Deep End of the Ocean." It made me cry. Well, I need some sleep. Good night!

Erin

APRIL, 1999 6:30 P.M.

I am in Wisconsin. Tomorrow is Easter. We will be spend-ing it with the whole family. Mom made sure I was ok with going. I am not going to miss out on seeing the rest of my family because Brian is going to be there. Why should I have to suffer? Allie is in Kentucky with one of her friends for Easter. My Aunt Jenny, the one who I was a flower girl for, is having her baby any day now. I think it is going to be a girl. My other aunt is due in September with twins. She is very excited. So I will have three new cousins this year.

Erin

APRIL, 1999 10:00 P.M.

I got home tonight from Wisconsin after a long day at Easter. Like usual I hated it. I try not to let it affect me, but just seeing Brian brings back horrible memories. My nightmares leave me getting little sleep at night. I have decided maybe if I try to be happy things will get better. In a way ignore these feelings I have inside and maybe they will just disappear. School is tomorrow. I must get some sleep. I am doing much better in math now that my teacher is gone. I went from failing to getting a B.

Erin

MAY, 1999 2:00 A.M.

My pulse is racing and my face is pouring sweat. I feel like I just ran forever. I have just woken up from a horrible nightmare. I was being chased through a house until I made my way outside and then a man with a dog was chasing after me. I eventually stumble to the ground where I am being attacked not by the dog, but instead by a man. He begins ripping off my clothes and raping me. The dream gets blurry and then I wake up. I now lay staring at my ceiling wondering when my life will get back to normal or if it ever will. I am going to close my eyes and try falling back asleep to the memories of my childhood before I was abused. The childhood when all I remember were the sounds of my laughter and not my cries.

Erin

JULY, 1999 12:10 A.M.

I know it has been awhile since I wrote. Well, things have been going ok, I guess, but that is because I've been holding in all my pain. Well, tonight things hit me pretty hard. I went to camp this month and made a lot of new friends and had fun, but at night my top bunk bed I lay looking out the window gazing at all the stars with tears pouring from my eyes. The memories are so fresh. I have put on a few pounds over the summer because food is my way of comforting myself. My mom is always available to talk to, but she is still having a hard time dealing with what happened to Allie and me. I still hear her crying in my dad's arms at night or crying on the phone to her friends. My mom's main purpose in being a stay-at-home mom was to be there and protect her girls from harm. So when she learned about what had happened behind closed doors for two years it was like her world around her came crashing down. I try turning to my friends, but they don't understand what I've been through. They listen, but they don't know what to say. I guess since they haven't been through it they don't really understand my pain. I am terrified to show my tears. I went to group and was about to break down and cry, but eventually got a grip on myself and stopped myself from crying. I guess what keeps me going every day is waiting for the day when I can look back on my life and realize how far I have really come. I look forward to the day I can wake up and truly be happy inside. For now though I continue to pretend.

Erin

JULY, 1999 10:30 P.M.

I wrote a poem today that reflects on a nightmare I had this week.

NIGHTMARE

I run through the night
In a panicked fright.
I feel him coming after me
I beg him to let me be.
He almost has me
And all I want is to be free
I feel him tackle me to the ground
And I wake from the horrible
Nightmare sound.

JULY, 1999 11:30 P.M.

I went to work with dad this week. I can't believe what he does every day. I could barely handle cleaning carpets for five minutes and he has been doing it before I was even born. I give him a whole lot of credit. Tonight mom, dad, Allie, and I played cards over at my dad's good friend's house. We actually sold the house to my dad's friend and we bought the house behind them. The game we played is with one card and you play with a dollar. Aces are the worst and kings are the best. In the end someone wins all the money. Allie won the game and won twenty dollars. Tomorrow is the picnic down at our beach and I hope I don't have to see Brian. It ruins my entire day when I have to see him. My fingers are crossed.

Erin

AUGUST, 1999 10:45 P.M.

I just got home from Wisconsin. There were a lot of people at the picnic including Brian. He was actually helping out. He was dipping the corn on the cob in butter and handing it to people. The corn is the best part of the meal, but there was no way I was walking over and getting a piece. My dad brought me back a piece, which was nice of him. I also dealt with a flashback while I was there. I didn't know how to control it so I jumped in the lake, which brought me back to reality. My grandparents rally around Brian like he is this wonderful grandson and it really hurts to see them act this way. They attend all his football games and brag about him like he is this wonderful grandson, which really gets me angry. Mom just explains to me that they are living in denial just like Brian's parents and other relatives. Anyway, it has been a long weekend and I need some sleep.

Erin

AUGUST, 1999 8:30 P.M.

My mom called Grandma today and told her we would no longer be attending family parties. My mom told her we have had enough of being blamed for something Brian did and everyone brushing it off like it was no big deal. Grandma just doesn't understand and feels she doesn't favor Brian, but we all see it. I just wish I could go to sleep and wake ten years from now with no memory of the past. It sounds so easy only if it were true. Instead I continue to struggle.

Erin

AUGUST, 1999 9:30 P.M.

I went and saw the movie "Sixth Sense" last night. It was a great movie. I had group tonight. We started off like we usually do telling about our highs and lows of the week then we played a game called two truths and a lie. You tell two things that are true about you and one lie. Everyone goes around and guesses the lie. It was a fun game. Going to group is the one time I actually feel connected. I am with people who care about me and understand what I've been through. When group was over Cathy talked to my mom outside. Cathy was telling my mom that the girls in the group really look up to me as a leader. Which was nice to hear.

Erin

AUGUST, 1999 11:00 P.M.

School is about to start. Allie and Emily will be with me this year at the same school. I hope I have friends in classes this year. I babysat my Aunt Jenny's new baby Abby this week. She was born at the end of April. She is a cute baby. I can't wait until the twins are born next month. Next week I am going out with a bunch of friends and going shopping for make up. Kassie and Stephanie are my two best friends. I brought them up to Wisconsin this month for a weekend and we had so much fun together. At night we got a little scared because the alarm clock kept going off. They both know the house is haunted so we were all terrified.

We went into town and walked around. My mom was looking at dresses while Stephanie, Kassie and I did our own shopping. Then we pretended that Kassie was deaf and she was walking around doing sign language, but she really wasn't signing anything that made sense. People were looking at us like we were crazy. We were having fun so it didn't matter what people thought. I am talking to Cathy next week. I think I need to open up with her more. I don't know what is holding me back from expressing myself. Well, Allie is sleeping in the same room as me and wants me to end this entry. So good-bye for now.

Erin

August, 1999 11:00 P.M.

I got my schedule for school and have no classes with any of my friends, which really had me upset. It is Saturday night and I am in Wisconsin. I went to this house on the water today with Allie and her friend. The house had a water trampoline and the owner let us jump on it. We were jumping off it and into the water. We then played king of the trampoline and tried pushing each other off into the water. It was so much fun. We also went tubing this weekend. All together it was a pretty good weekend right before school is to start. Good night!

Erin

September, 1999 8:30 P.M.

The school year has started and I already hate it. I did find out I have a lot of classes with my friend Chris who I went to elementary school with. He is in six of my classes. So we have been talking a lot. Caitlin is baking cupcakes for football players right now. She is a senior in high school this year. My group at the Advocacy Center ended and Allie and Mom are now in a group. They have a group for girls Allie's age and a parents' support group. I think my mom needed that. Caitlin has been trying to get me to open up to her, but I just don't know how to talk about my feelings. It is like I have this wall up that is preventing me from talking about it. Everything is just too hard to go into detail about. I still remember the night before my mom ever found out about the abuse. She was clueless on what was going on behind closed doors. And then I remembered the day she did find out. It looked like the life in her was sucked out. I try every day to push myself to get over it. I just don't know where to turn.

Erin

OCTOBER, 1999 11:30 P.M.

I don't pay attention in school anymore. I am not happy. All I hear are my screams in my nightmares, or the cries of the pain I've been through. My soul is a cold dark place. In a sense I feel dead inside. Too afraid to show my tears so I always look the other way. Since my silence has been broken and I am no longer carrying this secret alone, I still feel so alone and lost in the world. I feel I lost my voice at the same time Brian stole my innocence, robbed me of my childhood, and took my trust. I still am in search of my voice. Still hearing Brian's voice echoing through my head. Telling me over and over that it is our secret and no one will believe me if I tell. It is hearing these words over and over again that has me so afraid to talk about my past. The details are too painful bringing back horrible memories. Memories I can never erase.

Erin

DECEMBER, 1999 10:30 P.M.

Things haven't been good. I spent Thanksgiving at our house with my cousins from Michigan, which was fun, especially since we weren't with the family. Brian went down state for the high school football team and it was on TV. I saw him on TV cheering with his team after a touchdown. It hurts so bad to see myself suffering because of what he did as he goes on with his life. I am working on how to deal with the flashbacks and nightmares. I play music at night to put me to sleep, but it doesn't always work. The holidays are the hardest because a lot of the abuse happened during the holidays. This year I am looking forward to the holidays for once because we are spending it differently than years past.

Thanksgiving was spent with my mom's sister and kids. For Christmas Eve we are going over to my mom's friend's house that has two boys. So the holidays will be much better then years past. Anyway I have school tomorrow so I must get some sleep.

Erin

December, 1999 9:12 P.M.

I wrote grandma a letter a couple weeks ago expressing my feelings about how she has handled the situation with Brian. I told her how I felt she was favoring Brian and told her to stop being in denial. I told her how much it hurts me to see the family treat us the way they have, looking at my family as if we did something wrong. I told her to learn the truth before making assumptions. I got a call this morning and it was grandma asking me to go to lunch with her. I knew immediately why, and told her I would go. On the way to lunch grandma finally brought up the letter. She told me she doesn't feel she favors anyone and says she is staying out of it. She feels it is none of her business and treats all her grandkids equally. I felt very uncomfortable and told grandma that is the impression I've been getting.

She apologized and told me that if that is what I interpreted then she is sorry. She never meant to make it look that way. The conversation was short and at lunch we talked about other things. I just realized that my grandparents and my relatives are in denial and can't accept the fact that a sexual perpetrator is in the family. Someday they will learn the truth.

Erin

DECEMBER, 1999 11:15 P.M.

A flashback is starting to occur. It is all too difficult to handle. His eyes stare at me and I am flashing back to a time in January when he abused me. I am stuck in this memory and can't escape. I lay in the dark in his bedroom as he hurts me. I am screaming inside, but no one hears my silent screams. I am begging him to stop. The flashback eventually ends and I am rocking back and forth on my bed. I pull myself under the covers and cry myself to sleep.

Erin

DECEMBER, 1999 12:30 A.M.

I had a wonderful Christmas for the first time in years. Spending it with my mom's friend was the best thing for me. We exchanged presents with each other, had dinner together, played cards and even went next door and sang Christmas songs to the neighbors. It was a great night. When we got home we opened presents like usual and stayed up late. Grandpa and Grandma came the next day to see what we got. Christmas day mom made a turkey dinner and we stayed home and had our eighty-four-year-old neighbor over as well. We had some relatives show up Christmas day who brought my sisters and me presents. My sisters and I got the feeling they missed us because we are not there for the holidays. I wish I could be there because they're relatives I enjoy seeing, but having Brian there makes it very difficult for me. Brian never even apologized for his actions. Someday maybe he will.

Erin

DECEMBER, 1999 1:00 A.M.

Things have been a bit hectic around here. There is a surprise birthday party for my grandpa because he is turning seventy. We had no plans to attend because we don't go to family parties. Well the family really wants us there. The extended family members and friends of my grandparents would wonder why we weren't there and how can you explain that to other relatives that don't know about Brian? My Uncle Bill and Uncle John took my dad out to a bar tonight and they talked about the situation with Brian and the surprise party. They asked what would need to be done to have us at the party. My dad told them that Brian never apologized for his actions. They talked for a total of five hours. Now my Uncle Bill wants to talk to my mom about it. So they are going out tomorrow for lunch. I wonder what will happen.

Erin

Memories

"Healing takes courage, and we all have courage, even if we have to dig a little to find it."

—Tori Amos

JANUARY, 2000 11:00 A.M.

My heart is racing right now. Tonight Brian is going to apologize. Here is what happened. My mom went out yesterday with my Uncle Bill for lunch. At lunch Bill questioned my mom about what needs to be done so we would go to the surprise party on Sunday. Mom told him the girls want a meaningful apology. They talked at lunch for a long time. I didn't think much of it. I spent New Year's Eve last night with a bunch of friends at Melissa's house and spent the night there. I came home this morning on New Years Day and about ten minutes after I got home the phone rang. My dad answered and I overheard him say "Five-thirty tonight at your house." Then he hung up and went upstairs and told my mom we are meeting over at Bill's house where Brian wants to apologize tonight. Mom told Allie and me and asked us if we are okay with that. I told mom I was nervous and she said that was normal. So now it is the waiting game until tonight. I am so scared and don't know what is going to happen. I haven't spoken to Brian in over a year and a half. I will write tonight about what happens.

Erin

JANUARY, 2000 12:45 A.M.

What a night for the first day of the New Year. On the way over to my Uncle Bill's my stomach was in knots. Bill lives right next door to Brian. So my aunt, uncle and Brian all came over to Bill's. Walking in the door I could see Brian's reflection in the window. We all met in the kitchen and Bill asked us all to go downstairs. We all took a seat on a couch or chair in the room. I sat across the room from Brian. It was really uncomfortable for me. Bill asked who wanted to start. Lifting his head Brian looked at Allie and me and said he was sorry for what he did. He said if he could take it back he would. Mom said a few things and then Bill asked Allie and me if there was anything we wanted to say. Allie didn't want to say anything and I just said I hope you learned your lesson and will never hurt anyone the way you've hurt me. Mom spoke a little to Aunt Mary and you could sense the tension between them. The meeting was short and ended with us talking about Grandpa's surprise party tomorrow. Brian, my aunt, and uncle all left soon after. We waited for Uncle Bill who was going out to dinner with us. At dinner Bill asked my parents, Allie and me how we felt about the meeting. My mom said she thought it went well and we all agreed with her. I am just glad it is over and done with. I hope I can move on with my life now and not be affected by the past. It is very late and I need sleep.

Erin

JANUARY, 2000 10:00 P.M.

Grandpa's surprise party was fun. It was held at this big banquet place. Grandpa was told it was a celebration for Brian and his football team. Which doesn't surprise me that they used Brian. After all he is the favored grandson. When we pulled up, a sign outside the place read "Congratulations football players". When grandpa walked in everyone shouted surprise and he was very shocked. We ate dinner and a bunch of people got up and talked about grandpa. Although Brian has apologized, things still feel the same. I hope things will get better. I just hope the apology was sincere and not just for show so we would go to the surprise party. I have a feeling family members convinced Brian to apologize so we would come. That is the reason I didn't tell him I forgive him last night. Unless I truly know he is sorry, he will not hear that from me. My birthday is coming up soon, I will be fifteen. I am having a party with a bunch of friends over. I am inviting Kelly who was in group with me at the Children's Advocacy Center. Mom won't be at my party. She will be leaving for Michigan to visit her sisters. Dad is going to be hiding out in his bedroom leaving us alone. It should be a fun night. Anyway I am getting tired. I'll write more another time.

Erin

MARCH, 2000 12:40 A.M.

It has been awhile since I wrote in my journal. I have been holding a lot in. Things didn't get better like I hoped. I am trying not to show that I am struggling, but my teachers see it. They had a parent conference and talked to my parents about how down I have been. Mom explained a little to them about what I've been through. On top of that I'm struggling to stay on top of things at school. It just isn't easy. I really like my math teacher, Mrs. Verstat. Although I have never liked math she has had a huge impact on me this year. It is the one year I actually have received A's in math. Mrs. Verstat got class started a couple weeks ago and pulled me out in the hall. We talked for a long time. She asked me why I looked so down. I told her there are problems at home and school is a struggle. I explained to her that I feel my teachers doubt me because I do poorly on tests. Like I am slacker and don't give it my all. I told her I have so many dreams for my future, but I don't see it happening. With sisters who do so well in school as it comes so easy to them. Then there I am studying and I still struggle. Tears formed in my teacher's eyes and she told me I could be anything I wanted to be and not to let anyone stop me. She told me I had a lot of strengths and determination and just because I do poorly on tests isn't going to stop me from becoming successful. She told me a little bit about her years in school and how her sister was better in school than she was, but that didn't stop her from giving it her all. Mrs. Verstat said we could work together on anything I was struggling in. Eventually the bell rang and I had to get to my next class. I was very touched by my teacher's kind words to me. It is something that has made a deep impact on my outlook on life. She'll always have a special place in my heart.

Erin

MARCH, 2000 9:10 P.M.

I had the most exciting day. For years I wanted to go to an Oprah show. I have written her for years and finally got the call I have been waiting for. I wrote in awhile back about the topic of teens and depression. I wrote how I struggled with being depressed. They invited my mom and me to sit in the audience and watch the show. It wasn't the happiest show to see, but the whole day in general was an experience I will never forget. Driving to the city and then sitting in the audience with front row seats. It was all too good to be true. I also got a sweatshirt, hat, and t-shirt that say "Oprah Winfrey Show." I saw Oprah in person, which was much better then watching her on the TV. Mom took the day off work to go to the show. Mom also pulled me out of school for the entire day. After the show we went to lunch across the street. It was an altogether fun day.

Erin

MARCH, 2000 7:40 P.M.

I am in my bedroom and don't even want to leave. I just want to go to sleep and never wake up again. I feel so far removed from the world around me. I feel like I am in some other world. Half the time I am somewhere else in my head reliving memories of the abuse. I can't remember the last time I felt true happiness. I wish all the icky feelings inside would just go away. The flashbacks I continue to have and the nightmares that keep me up at night. It is like I am still running from Brian. I pray so hard that God will help me. I want to live in the present, not the past.

Erin

APRIL, 2000 9:00 P.M.

I am getting ready for bed, but I'm not tired at all. I have been coming home from school and sleeping all the time. It is the only time I feel good. No one understands my pain. I am so sad and feel so lost in this world. Mom sat down with me and told me she wanted me to talk to her about my feelings. I told mom that I wanted to have a healthy relationship with her and tell her about the good things, not the bad. Lately I've been having thoughts of ending my life. I feel I don't belong here anymore. I would be much happier with God than anywhere else. I just couldn't put my family through that. They have been through enough. I wouldn't want to cause them any more pain, but I just don't know where to turn. I feel locked up inside. Like I am living in a prison that I can't escape. My dreams are what keep me alive. Dreaming of going to college, getting married, and having children. Good night!

Erin

APRIL, 2000 7:30 P.M.

I just got home from Wisconsin. It was Easter weekend.

We all went down to grandma and grandpa's except mom. She stayed at the house. She doesn't appreciate the way she is treated by my dad's family. Brian was there and I didn't even look at him. I avoided him all together. I feel so uncomfortable around the family. Like everything is all an act. They are in so much denial about the past. Majority of them believe it was something minor. I didn't stay long, just long enough to get something to eat and leave. I began to have a flashback of the night in grandma and grandpa's condo in Wisconsin. Thinking back now I wonder how long Brian was abusing me before I woke up. It is something that lingers in the back of my head all the time. I have tried to block out so many memories, but there are too many to forget.

Erin

JUNE, 2000 11:05 PM

My junior high years are finally over. High school is the next big step for me. I remember my first day of kindergarten like it was yesterday. I can't believe how fast time has gone. My parents enjoy reminding me of the little terror I was as a kid. I turned to my first grade teacher one day and said, "You have gray hair." Ever since then she has been dying her hair. Another time I said something inappropriate was when I told this same teacher that she had long toenails. She had slip on shoes and took them off when reading a story. We went on our eighth grade trip to navy pier and went on the biggest boat on Lake Michigan. We got our pictures taken, ate lunch, and danced. It was a great way to end the year. We then had graduation that took place at the high school. Now it will be off to high school at the end of August. I am really nervous for high school. On top of that Brian will be there. He will be a senior, which will really suck. His parents held him back an extra year when he was going into kindergarten, otherwise he would already graduated. I am going to have to face him every day at school. I really don't know how I am going to do it. It has been hard enough trying to hold everything in, but having to hold everything in and face him every day seems impossible. I don't even want to think about it.

Erin

JUNE, 2000 12:00 P.M.

I went to Wisconsin today for the weekend. The weather is just starting to warm up. My whole family had a campfire tonight. The stars were so bright. It was one of those nights I could just fall asleep under the stars. It is so peaceful and relaxing. If I wait long enough I can see a shooting star across the sky. The people that live behind us are coming up tomorrow. We are probably going out to dinner with them and then playing cards. We also spend Fourth of July with them. All my relatives go to this resort and eat dinner. My parents, sisters and I go to the same resort, but barbequed at home before we went. We sat by my dad's high school friends and watch fireworks. This is one holiday we always spend without the other relatives. For so long now I have been pushing so much pain down that I am to the point that I am numb inside. Life just seems to get harder as the days go by.

Erin

AUGUST, 2000 10:30 P.M.

I played cards tonight with Allie and mom. This summer has been going ok. The weather has been great. This month will be pretty hectic. My parents are preparing to send Caitlin off to college. She is going to University of Illinois. She will be studying elementary education. So she won't be living at home anymore. Then I will be making the big step to high school, which will be a new experience for me. I hope I do well in high school. My schedule came and I have classes with some people I know. I have lunch with a bunch of my friends, which will be nice. I just hope I don't see Brian. He is pretty well known around school, since he is captain of the football team. I hope they lose every game. Anyway I need to walk Chance one more time before going to bed. Night!

Erin

AUGUST, 2000 9:15 P.M.

High school will start tomorrow. I am really nervous and can't fall asleep. It will be weird seeing my mom in the cafeteria all the time. She leaves later than me in the morning. A family friend is taking me to school everyday. I go to her youth group with her and her brother and sisters every week. She has been nice enough to offer to take me to school every morning. Mom will take me home since she gets off the same time I do. I am signed up for private driver training classes. It is a three-week course and then it is just a matter of waiting until I am sixteen to get my license. The freedom to drive will be fun. I have to get up early so I better get to sleep. Good night!

Erin

OCTOBER, 2000 8:45 P.M.

High school has been going ok. I am well adjusted, but struggling with flashbacks. We recently had a high school pep rally in the gym and during the pep rally the football players came out. My English teacher is the announcer during the pep rally and turned to the crowd and told everyone that the next person he is about to call up is a hero to our school. He then said could you give a loud cheer for captain of the football team, Brian. My stomach turned to knots and anger just filled me. How could they call him a hero? That is the last thing he should be considered. To make matters worse, a friend sitting next to me at the game asked if that was my cousin. I told her he was and she asked if I was proud of him. It just pissed me off even more. I couldn't believe thousands of people were cheering for Brian. If only they knew his past. I so badly wanted to get up and shout to the entire gymnasium what he put me through. Instead I sat there biting my tongue and holding back the tears. My night was ruined and I just wanted to get home and go to bed. I cried myself to sleep later that night.

Tonight I went out with my new friend, Sarah, who is also a freshman in high school. She is in my first hour study hall and second hour gym class. I told her about my past. She has been sitting with me at the pep rally and understood a little of my pain. I need to get started on English homework.

Erin

October, 2000 5:05 p.m.

I just got back from driver training. I learned up hill and down hill parking. It was very easy. We went driving afterwards. I am very uncomfortable in the car with my driving teacher. He and I are alone for an hour driving around. I often wonder if he is capable of hurting me the way Brain did.

I have another really good friend this year. Her name is Jackie and she has also had a rough past. She doesn't even live with her parents. She lives in a group home in my town. Her mother lost custody of her and her dad is dead. She is very depressed, but we try to lean on each other for support. She is one person I feel understands me. She is in my English class. We pass notes all the time. I really like my English teacher, Mr. Berns. The scary thing is my dad had Mr. Berns as a teacher when he went to my high school. He is a great teacher. I am thinking about trying out for the bowling team at high school. Just something fun to do and keep me busy. Well, mom needs help making dinner so I will end this here.

Erin

October, 2000 1:20 a.m.

I just woke up from a terrible nightmare and can't fall back asleep. I have school in the morning and I'm going to be exhausted. Brian was chasing me in my dream and I kept running and running on this road surrounded by cornfields. It seemed the more I ran the longer the road got and Brain was getting closer and closer. I eventually fell flat on my face and Brian began attacking me and I immediately woke up sweating and shaking. I can't even get a good night's sleep without being haunted by my past. I just wish I could erase everything and start over. Sigh.

Erin

November, 2000 9:20 p.m.

Caitlin is coming home for the weekend. This will be her first time home since she left for college. I made the bowling team and have my first meet tomorrow. We bowl six days a week until the first week in February. We do get time off during Christmas but that is it. I need something to keep me busy and focused so hopefully this will be the trick. My mom is trying to get me to open up and talk to her. I have trouble talking about my past to just about anyone. It is all too painful to talk about. I wish I could curl up in a ball and shut myself off from the world around me and wake up ten years from now. If only it were that easy. I really wonder how other people handle what I've been through. If they struggle with the same thing I do day in and day out. It is just unfair.

Erin

NOVEMBER, 2000 8:30 P.M.

I am in Wisconsin sitting in the basement by the fire with a cup of tea. Allie and my dad are behind me playing foosball. I don't know where I am going to sleep tonight. The upstairs is haunted and the bedroom by my parents' room has a lot of bugs in it. Dad tells me to sleep on the bunk beds in the basement because it is warm down here with the fire. Dad doesn't know that those bunk beds represent a lot of pain for me. The beds used to belong to Brian and his brother. Brian abused me on one of the beds. I would rather sleep on the hard, cold concrete then sleep on one of those beds. The beds were given to us before I came out about the abuse. My parents didn't think about the beds as being a problem for me. They don't even know I was abused on one of them.

One of my teachers is concerned about me and talked to one of the school social workers. She set up a time next week for me to come in and talk to her. I really don't know if I will be able to talk about anything. I walk the halls with my head held down feeling worthless. My flashbacks have become more frequent now that Brian is in school with me. I still push all the pain down and try to ignore it all. I guess the hardest part is looking back on my life and remembering the days when I was a happy kid. Just when I thought things couldn't get any better they took a turn for the worse when the abuse began. The day my innocence, trust, and childhood was stolen from me. I have to figure out where I am going to sleep tonight.

Erin

NOVEMBER, 2000 12:30 A.M.

It is Thanksgiving night and I am just glad it is over. Thanksgiving is the most uncomfortable family holiday of the entire year. I dread it every year. It is worse than any other holiday. I think it has to do with the whole meaning behind Thanksgiving about being thankful. I can't even think about being thankful sitting through an entire meal across from Brian. I feel nothing but disgust. It is all meaningless and pointless to me and I hate every moment of it. I don't even enjoy eating turkey. I sit there wondering what is running through his mind. His football team didn't go very far this year and I was thrilled. The only time I will ever cheer on another team besides my high school is when Brian is playing. His season is finally over. Well, it has been a long day and I plan to sleep in tomorrow.

Erin

Nightmares

"What lies behind us and what lies before us are tiny matters compared to what lies within us."

—Henry Thoreau

JANUARY, 2001 7:45 A.M.

It is the first day back from winter break. These days are always the hardest trying to get back to the swing of things. Our break went by too fast. Jackie hasn't been in school for over a month. I learned that she tried killing herself and was placed in a hospital. We both have talked about suicide, but I never thought she would go through with it. I heard she is ok, but has been in a behavioral hospital for the past month. I wonder if she will be back in school today? I had a good Christmas. I got my school jacket. I spent New Year's with my friends and was up until five in the morning. I have bowling practice after school today until 5:30 then I will have homework to do. Sarah is passing me a note so I am going to end this and read it. She sits two seats in front of me. We have been sneaky when passing notes. It isn't allowed.

Erin

JANUARY, 2001 7:50 A.M.

I am in study hall once again. Jackie still isn't back at school. I heard something very disturbing on the bus after school yesterday waiting to go to the bowling alley. A group of girls on the team were in the back of the bus talking and someone brought up perverted people at our school. A senior and caption of the team began telling a group of girls about a party she went to with her friend back in October. She said a senior guy who was at this party got her friend drinking and led her upstairs to a bedroom. She hadn't noticed her friend was not around until awhile later so she went searching for her and eventually discovered her upstairs struggling in a bedroom with this guy who was trying to rape her. She stormed in and got him off her. She said she and her friend and her left immediately and never told anyone. Everyone listening to the story was dead silent until everyone started to ask who the guy was. She went on to say a senior named Brain Nelson. A lump formed in my throat and I was in shock. Over and over again I told myself I did not just hear that. He had once again tried hurting another girl. It hit me right there that his apology was all bullshit and it was all for show. He is still the creep he has always been. Then another girl on the team who has known me since I was in elementary school called to me and said, "Isn't that your cousin?" The bus grew silent and all eyes were on me. There was no lying and I just admitted that he was. The captain of the team apologized over and over. I told her there was no need for her to apologize for something that is true. The whole ride to the bowling alley I sat in silence staring out the window holding back my tears. I could hear the whispers of the other teammates talking about it from the back of the bus. Just before we arrived at the bowling alley, another girl came up and sat next to me. She told me that she was really sorry. I told her not to be. I bowled terrible the whole day and was not picked to bowl this Thursday at the meet. When I got home I told mom about the conversation on the bus. She wasn't one bit surprised. It is upsetting to know someone like that can just get away with what he has done. Life can be very unfair.

Erin

FEBRUARY, 2001 7:45 P.M.

It is finally official! I can drive without parents. I got my license today after school. My birthday was Friday and I turned 16. I couldn't believe how easy the driving test was. I didn't feel like I was under any pressure either. The lady who took me out for my driving test was really nice. I just acted really calm and talked to her as if feeling I was confident, even though I was trembling inside. Then she brought me back early, and I hadn't done half the things I was supposed to do for the driving test. I seriously thought I failed it until I pulled up and parked the van and she told me I passed. I was holding my breath there for a while. Now it is time to look for a job so I can buy a car. I am thinking of looking for a job at a daycare. I am going to the grocery store to pick up a few things. I love the freedom of being able to drive. Beep! Beep!

Erin

FEBRUARY, 2001 9:30 P.M.

I was hired today at a daycare. I will be making six dollars an hour. When I went in for my interview I acted really confident the same way I did when I took the driving test, but I was really nervous. The lady who interviewed me who is also the director was a younger lady. I am not too sure about the owner. He seems a little uptight, but I won't make any assumptions until I really get to know him. I peeked in the babies' room and there are some babies that are so tiny and they are all so adorable. I am going to start in the room with the one-year-olds, which is a fun age group. My hours are right after school until closing time which is at six P.M. I start this Monday and work Monday through Friday. Dad tells me he will double the money I have in the bank come summer to buy a car.

Erin

MARCH, 2001 10:40 P.M.

Other than all the pain and anger I am trying to hide, things have been going pretty good. This past month so much has happened. I received an award at school, which a teacher must give two students through the year. I was called to the principal's office and received the award, which gets me into all the school events free and all the school dances free except for the prom. The funny thing about that is I'm going to the prom even though I know I am only a freshman. I think it is really crazy. At the same time I am so excited. Well it happened like this. There is this guy named Steve who is a junior. My mom introduced me to him at school. I guess from what mom tells me he is always talking to her.

I've known him for about two weeks and he asked me to come to a high school basketball game with him. This year our team is doing awesome and hopefully we will go to state. So I went with my parents and sister to the game, but met up and sat with Steve and his friends. It was a really fun night. What was really exciting is we won with a basket as the buzzer went off in the fourth quarter. Steve took off his shirt, and I noticed he had another white shirt on underneath it. I didn't see it at first. I soon saw people around me giggling. I was trying to see what they were looking at. Right before my eyes written in red marker were the words "Erin, will you go to prom with me?" I was shocked and embarrassed at the same time. I immediately told him I would. I later found out mom knew all day that he was going to ask me. After the game we all went out to eat with a bunch of players from the team. That is when Steve asked me about dating him. I was taken back by the question because I was still in shock over getting asked to prom. I eventually told him I would be more than happy to date him. At the same time my stomach was in a knot inside. Not knowing if dating him would trigger me. So far it hasn't been a trigger.

Today I was over at his house watching a movie, then we talked for two hours. He is an only child so he has the house to himself other then his parents. In our two-hour talk I told him about my past. It wasn't easy to talk about, but I wanted to make sure he knew so he could understand that things might be difficult for me. Steve was disgusted when I told him, especially because he knows who Brian is. At around seven tonight his mom drove me home. Steve walked me to the front door where he gave me my first kiss. I was not prepared at all for it but it was a special experience. Well, I am going to have good dreams tonight.

Erin

MARCH, 2001 10:00 P.M.

I went down state with a bunch of friends for the state basketball game and no one expected us to win, but we did.

We won the state championship for basketball. It was such an exciting weekend. Steve found me right after we won. He was so excited and started kissing me in front of my friends. It was a really exciting weekend. I have a lot of fun hanging out with my friends. Prom is just around the corner. It will be here before I know it. I know another freshman going to the prom, which will be nice. I still have to find a dress. I went to the mall, but didn't see anything I liked. We are visiting Caitlin at U of I next month so I might look at the mall there. I'll find something.

Erin

APRIL, 2001 8:30 P.M.

I just got up here in Wisconsin. I've been very busy, haven't had time to journal much. I am working five days a week at the daycare. I work in the nursery with the newborns all the time. I love being with the little babies. Other than work, I have been getting ready for the prom. Things are not going well between Steve and me. I will probably break up the relationship. I'm just not at a point in my life to be in a relationship. I think we are better off friends. Last week I went to the University of Illinois and visited my sister Caitlin. She told mom while we were visiting her that she is planning on finishing up this year and then moving to California. Mom wasn't too happy to hear any of it. Allie and I spent most of the time down in the pool at the hotel. I need to go walk Chance. Tomorrow will make it four years that I've had Chance. I can't believe how fast time has gone by.

Erin

MAY, 2001 10:15 P.M.

I had a great time at the prom this past weekend. Although Steve and I are not dating any more, it was a great night. We went down to navy pier and went on a boat for a couple hours. The city was so beautiful at night. Steve and I stood on the top level of the boat where plenty of students go so they can get close or cuddle with their dates. When we got up there I saw Brian and immediately got a knot in my stomach. I started to panic and felt a flashback approaching. Steve and I didn't stay up there much longer after that. I just wish I could live my life without being reminded of my childhood all the time. It seems no matter which way I go I run into my past some way or another. It bothers me terribly. I just want to move on with my life.

Erin

MAY, 2001 8:30 P.M.

Summer is approaching and I am really looking forward to it. I will be working all summer at the daycare saving up for a car. I am really enjoying being with the babies all day. They are so innocent and adorable. I don't know how parents leave their infants all day. I could never hand over my baby every day. I want to have many children when I find the right man. Allie will be in high school next year with me. She is looking forward to the new change in schools. My freshman year has gone by so fast. One thing I hate most about summer is I see Brian all the time in Wisconsin. It bothers me so much to cross paths with him up there. He is nothing but a painful reminder that I have to face. My mom is calling for me so I better end this here.

Erin

JULY, 2001 9:00 P.M.

Two days ago when I came back from work I pulled in the driveway to see a car I didn't recognize. It turned out to be the car my dad bought for me. I have never been so excited. I paid for half and dad paid the other half. It looks like a brand new car. The neighbors were over taking a look at it too. It has a sunroof, CD player, and leather interior. I drove up to Wisconsin Friday night with Allie. I just want to drive around everywhere. I have worked so hard for it. I spend my week at home working while mom and Allie go back and forth from Illinois to Wisconsin. Allie has cheerleading practice twice a week. I stay home with Dad in Illinois. I miss being in Wisconsin though. I'm going to go get ice cream with Allie.

Erin

JULY, 2001 12:30 A.M.

I think a lot about where I will be in ten years. Will I still carry around the pain I feel everyday. Will I still hold on to the anger and hate I feel towards Brian? I feel like I have been running for years, but can't understand why I am running. I am safe now and no longer being hurt, but that doesn't make it easier when it comes to the memories of the abuse that constantly are affecting my life. There are so many other children each day who become a new victim to this horrible abuse. It breaks my heart to know someone can do something so horrible to an innocent child. I am too afraid to express my pain so I hold a lot of it in hoping it will eventually go away. I pray daily that God will help me through another day. For now it is time for bed. I will write more some other night.

Erin

July, 2001 10:30 p.m.

I have had a busy weekend. I babysat Saturday night for an adorable little girl named Molly. She is two years old and full of energy. I also played a huge game of softball with family and friends at a field up the street from my house. Caitlin is leaving soon. She has been living here all summer with her friend Christy that she met at the University of Illinois. They are both moving to California together next week in hopes of becoming famous. She wants to be on television so much. The chances of that ever happening are slim, but who knows she may just be discovered. Only time will tell. I look up to Caitlin for advice. She is one person I can express my feelings to. I feel Caitlin really understands me. She is the kind of sister that you can pick up the phone and call in the middle of the night if you need to. I am back home again in Illinois. I have to work in the morning so I better get some sleep. Those little babies can really wear me out after awhile, but I still love them. It is a great job. Night!

Erin

September, 2001 11:00 p.m.

It is a Saturday night and I am up in Wisconsin watching Saturday Night Live with Allie. Last month our neighbor Bob across the street died. He was only in his fifties. I found out when I came back from the beach and I began crying when I heard the news. He was such a great neighbor. Whenever Allie or I had a fundraiser, Bob always went out of his way and bought almost everything. He is really going to be missed.

Allie is getting adjusted to high school. She really is enjoying it and meeting new people. I played cards tonight with mom and Allie. I ended up winning. I no longer work at the daycare. I quit in the middle of August. It just became too much to handle. I really miss the babies. It was so hard to say good-bye. I was going to quit in November anyway because bowling starts, but it was still hard to leave. Well, I got another whole school year ahead of me. Freshman year went faster then I expected. Homecoming is coming up and I want to ask this junior boy I know. His mom works at the school, too. His name is Ryan and he is really a nice guy. Caitlin is living in California and is enjoying it. She actually made it on the Disney channel for a countdown to a song she sang while on the beach. She got her fifteen seconds of fame. Allie fell asleep and I better go wake her and get to bed myself.

Erin

OCTOBER, 2001 9:15 P.M.

School year has been going by faster then I expected. It is already the end of October. I am really looking forward to wearing my grandma costume for Halloween at school again this year. Homecoming was good and I ended up going with Ryan. It was a fun night. I am talking to an intern social worker at our school this year. Her name is Miss P. She is really nice and understanding. She in fact graduated from my high school a couple years ago. She is also helping run a group for girls who have been sexually abused. It has been going well and it is nice to be able to relate with other girls who can understand better then some of my friends who have never experienced what I went through. I don't talk much. It is difficult for me to express the abuse. I don't know what holds me back. My sleep has been a lot worse than usual. I struggle with nightmares and wake up terrified too afraid to go back to sleep. Other days I don't even want to get out of bed. I just hold out hope that things will get better.

Erin

OCTOBER, 2001 8:30 P.M.

I had a rough day today. I've bottled so much up inside me I feel like I am going to explode. I've been having suicidal thoughts and fantasies. I just don't see my life getting any easier. It just seems to get harder each day. Just getting out of bed is a challenge because I don't know what lies ahead of me for the day. I am sick of the daily struggle I face. I just want to be happy.

Erin

NOVEMBER, 2001 2:15 A.M.

I had a horrible nightmare tonight. I was being beaten and raped. I felt like I was running forever until I finally fell and was attacked. I woke up sweating and panicked. I now can't stop crying. I just want to be normal and not be affected by my past. I can't escape it anywhere I go. I just feel like I try to hide all the pain, but it is getting me nowhere. Mom always tries to talk to me, but I have trouble opening up. The abuse is such a sensitive issue for me. Not something I can just come out and talk about. I live in so much fear and anger. I feel I can't trust anyone. Not even people I love and call family. This entire experience I've been through as a child has really had a huge effect on me and has made me grow up a lot faster. I feel like I tip toe around in life not knowing if I will ever be hurt again. Wondering if I can even trust myself. I carry so much guilt. Like everything is my fault. Thanksgiving is coming soon and I look at it as the worst day of the entire year. Out of all the holidays Thanksgiving is the hardest. Having to sit across from Brian and pretend to be one big family and be thankful on top of it. To me I look at the entire day as one big joke. I'm happy when I can go home and see my dog Chance get excited over the leftover turkey I brought him. That is the highlight of my Thanksgiving. I just hope it goes by quick this year. I can only put on a fake act for so long.

Erin

NOVEMBER, 2001 11:15 P.M.

I went and saw the musical "Fame" tonight with my mom. A friend of ours was in it. I also saw some girls from my high school in the play. I am really tired right now and ready for bed. Tomorrow I am going to Wisconsin with my friend Sarah. It should be a fun day. I will write more when I come home tomorrow.

Erin

NOVEMBER, 2001 11:00 P.M.

I had so much fun today. I forgot about all my pain and anger today. I went up to Wisconsin with Sarah and her family. The house we visited was not too far from my summer house. We had dinner at their friend's house. We went out on a golf cart in the dark. Sarah and I took turns driving it. There was plenty of land to ride around on. On the way home we were exhausted and both fell asleep until her dad slammed on the breaks when a deer ran in front of the car. I am falling asleep just writing this. Night!

Erin

NOVEMBER, 2001 1:15 A.M.

I just woke from another nightmare again. I'm always afraid to go back to sleep because the dream starts back up where it last left off. I barely get any sleep, which is affecting me at school and making it hard to concentrate. It has been three years. Why does it still affect me? Well, I Hope to try getting some sleep. I hope journaling will help ease my anxiety.

NOVEMBER, 2001 4:05 A.M.

It is four in the morning and I still have not gone back to sleep. I am wide-awake. My nightmare was about being chased by Brian and I awaken just as I jumped off a cliff. I woke up and felt like I was screaming. Well there is no point in trying to get some sleep now. My alarm clock will be going off in about an hour. I will just lay here counting the glow-in-the-dark stars on my ceiling.

Erin

DECEMBER, 2001 1:30 A.M.

It is late out. I had another terrible Thanksgiving. I can't stand being there with everyone pretending everything is normal. Having to sit across from Brian at the same table as my stomach turns to knots. I kept my distance from the rest of the family counting down the hours until another family holiday is behind me. The men sit watching football, the woman all sit chatting at a table, and the children run around playing. Then there I am sitting off in the corner by myself dreading every minute of it. I now sit here starring at my ceiling wondering when I will fall back asleep. The school social worker, Miss P, recommended warm milk. It was working for a while there, but I'm back to tossing and turning through the night. I had a dream tonight of being chased through a cornfield. I am running until I trip and sprain my ankle. I continue to run with a limp until I run right into Brian and I wake up sweating. Another sleepless night!

Erin

December, 2001 10:30 p.m.

I just want to be happy. I want all these sad feelings inside to go away. I feel so down and lost. My sleeping patterns are awful. My focus is on other unimportant things. I really don't know what to do with myself. I just want to be a teenager going through average teenage days. Mrs. P wants me to talk to my mom about getting me on antidepressants and seeing a therapist. Mom thinks I have moved on with my life and I don't want to drag her down with my pain.

I had a good weekend. I went babysitting down in Chicago with Allie. We watched our twin cousins together in a hotel with an incredible view of the city. I must be getting some sleep. I have another long day ahead of me.

Erin

December, 2001 1:03 a.m.

Christmas is closing in and my anxiety is getting intense. Another holiday I must face. The worst part is it is for two days we are with the family. Christmas Eve and Christmas day. Tonight I went to a Christmas party with my sister Caitlin. It was at the home of a friend of ours from Wisconsin. The party was at her house in Illinois. At the party there were a bunch of other girls from our Wisconsin beach association. It was a pretty interesting party. I got to meet a lot of new people. We didn't get home until now so I am exhausted and need some sleep. I'll write more tomorrow which is Christmas Eve.

CHRISTMAS EVE, 2001 12:30 P.M.

It is Christmas Eve. Mom is downstairs baking cookies. Allie and I have been helping her. She makes tons of Christmas cookies each year. Caitlin is out doing last minute shopping. Dad is working out at the health club and then has a few things to pick up at the store. We are going over to my uncle's house around seven tonight. I look forward to coming home around midnight to open our presents. Mom is calling for me. She must need my help in the kitchen. Got to run!

Erin

DECEMBER, 2001 12:25 A.M.

Christmas was another dreadful holiday. We spent the evening going to my uncle's house where all our other relatives were. My grandparents have a friend that comes over dressed like Santa Clause and hands out presents to all the grandchildren. This year I asked for scrapbook materials. I got a huge box full of stickers, colored paper, and a scrapbook. I haven't had time to make anything just yet, but am looking forward to it when I can. I think I will make my first scrapbook on the trip we are taking in March. We are going to Colorado to go skiing. I am really looking forward to that. I've never skied in Colorado before so it will be a new experience for me. I am just about finished up with another bowling season behind me. Our last meet is right before my birthday. Tomorrow night we are celebrating my grandpa's birthday. I don't know how I survive these family events. Another year just about behind me as another one approaches. I was able to distance myself from Brian the whole night. Christmas day was dreadful. It is very similar to Thanksgiving. We all go to grandma's and have a big Christmas dinner together. The only difference from Thanksgiving and Christmas is they have a different meaning. I like the meaning behind Christmas more. I spent a lot of time playing with my younger cousins in the back bedroom where I wasn't surrounded by the rest of the family. With a new year just around the corner I want to start off with a new year's resolution. My resolution is the same as it has been for years. I want to move on with my life and become a stronger and better person. A part of my childhood was robbed. My innocence was taken from me. I can't let Brian take any more. Someday I hope to confront Brian. Let him know just how much pain he has caused me.

Erin

Scars

*"The cuts on my arms will eventually fade,
but the scar on my life will be there forever."*

—Erin Merryn

January, 2002 9:30 p.m.

I just try numbing out so much pain. Pain I am too afraid to face. Tears stream down my cheeks. Life just isn't the same. I often wonder what my point in life is. Really, what is my purpose in life?

Erin

January, 2002 6:00 p.m.

I talked to Miss P. today about the holidays. I told her how much it bothers me that my grandparents have supported Brian so much through his high school years. I love my grandparents, but have so much anger at how they pretend our family is perfect and Brian did no wrong. It makes me wonder what other families deal with in situations like mine. I'm a sixteen year old who just wants to move on with my life. Brian took so much from me already. I don't understand why the past continues to affect me. He already robbed me of my childhood. I can't let him rob me of my teenage years. I just don't know what I have to do to let go of all the pain. Pain I keep trying to bury, but feel it trying to come out. I try talking to my friends, but they don't understand what I've been through. They try to act supportive, but I get the sense that they just don't know what to say. The truth is they don't. They have never experienced the abuse I've been through to understand. I guess that is why I am feeling so alone in my life. I feel like I must come up with the answers within myself. I have to do some digging and search my soul to heal it. The problem is I'm too afraid to search. Instead I want to push it away hoping it will one day not be there. It is the hope that keeps me going every day.

Erin

FEBRUARY, 2002 11:00 P.M.

I'm seventeen years old now. I celebrated my birthday this past weekend. For my birthday I took my friend Sarah skiing in Wisconsin. It was her first time skiing so she was new to it. We took a bunch of pictures and had a blast. We skied almost all day and then went out to dinner for pizza where I opened my presents. I didn't have pizza instead I had shrimp. One thing I received was a bunch of scratch-off lottery tickets. While scratching them to see if I won, I heard dad making negative comments, telling me how lottery tickets are nothing but a waste of money. I had a total of seven to scratch. On the first two I won nothing. On the third one I won two dollars. The fourth one was the one I was waiting for. I scratched it and got three like amounts to win forty dollars. I looked at dad and asked him if it still wasn't worth it. All he could tell me is I got lucky. When I was all done I had a total of forty-four dollars. I ended up winning another two dollars on my last ticket. So I was pretty excited. When we got back to the house Sarah and I didn't stay up long. We were both exhausted from skiing and fell asleep immediately. We came home early Sunday because Sarah had to be somewhere. I am going right now to go get my pictures developed from the weekend. I'll write more another time.

Erin

MARCH 2002 8:30 P.M.

It's been four years this week since the last terrible night Brian nearly raped me. It still feels like it was just yesterday. There are so many details of that terrible night that I can't erase. Remembering Brian holding me down and me unable to free myself. Having his hands all over my body. I must end this here before I become too emotional. It's too painful!

Erin

MARCH 2002 10:00 P.M.

I began to write a poem today in Biology class. I was really supposed to be watching a video, but it was too boring. I just finished the poem tonight.

Lost Innocence

I love you
And trusted you too
Until one fateful day
You took it all away.
The touch of your hands.

Was only one of a man's.
Your weight was too strong.
You know what you did was wrong.
I wake up in the night
To your awful sight.
I sometimes look to the sky
And wonder why?
I've asked God plenty of times
Why you committed these crimes.
I remember watching the clock
As you pulled off your sock.
I wanted to run and hide
As you looked on in pride.
You pushed me on to carpeted floors.
Behind closed doors.
As you slid your hands down me
I struggle to be free.
You tell me not to tell
Just as I'm about to yell.
My body goes numb
Looking at your evil scum.
The night is over
But it didn't end there.
Of course you didn't care.
This went on for three years.
Which brings tears.
In the morning sunrise.
I dry the tears from my eyes.
Someday I'll get my way
Just watch, YOU'LL PAY!

APRIL 2002 9:20 P.M.

I just had the best spring break ever. My entire family went skiing in Colorado. We rented a condo that we stayed at. We drove fifteen hours to get there, but it was a fun drive. We spent three days skiing. It was my first time ever skiing on real mountains. Caitlin snowboarded the entire time and she wasn't too bad for a first timer. She started off skiing, but after rolling down the mountain head first, she was finished. My muscles in my body were so sore the first night after skiing. That a simple walk across the room was painful. We spent a lot of time in the hot tub. We had nice weather the entire time we were there. Being on the chair lifts was incredible. I've never felt so close to God before. You can see everything from the chair lifts. The mountains go on and on. I could even see another ski resort miles and miles away. Surrounding me were the green pine trees and the powder blue sky and the sun warming my face. I already look forward to next year when we go skiing again. The rest of my relatives went to Florida. They planned it out and rented a big million-dollar house on the ocean where they spent a week. Not a single person in the family invited my family. This is the second year they have gone without inviting us. We wouldn't go even if they did invite us, but they didn't even offer. I'd never consider being stuck in a house for a week with that family on a vacation. To me it sounds more like a nightmare. I don't let it eat away at me, though I wouldn't want to be around half that family to begin with. The family members I respect are the ones I have a relationship with. They are the ones that didn't take sides when everything came out about the abuse. I really look up to my Aunt Jenny. She is my favorite aunt and minded her own business when everything went downhill in the family, which is the reason I go over to her house so much and baby-sit for her. Anyway I could write a novel about how rude my relatives are, but it isn't worth my time. I have school in the morning and must get some sleep.

Erin

May 2002 10:00 P.M.

I just got home from babysitting for my Aunt Jenny tonight. She is due with her second baby in October. She is also moving next month. She needs more room with a new baby on the way. I am about to overcome my biggest fear next month. Allie and I are flying out to Texas to spend time with my aunt and uncle and cousins. I have been terrified to fly since I was young. I still can't believe I am going to do it. We are leaving the week after school gets out and spending a week and a half there. My aunt tells me she has a lot of fun stuff planned for us when we come. I can hear a plane flying over my house right now. I am putting it in God's hands. He'll keep me safe!

Erin

May, 2002 11:45 P.M.

Yesterday I went to my Aunt Jenny's house for my cousin's birthday. Everyone in the family was there including Brian. Brian brought his girlfriend with him. I kept my distance from him and stayed in a completely different room from him the entire day. When he looked at me I made sure to give him no eye contact. I won't give him the time of day. He left early, thank God; I don't know how much more I could handle being in the same house with him. It's about a week until I leave for Texas. I have never been so nervous.

Erin

JUNE 2002 11:48 P.M.

Tomorrow is the day I've been dreading for a long time. I leave for the airport at six in the morning. I can't fall asleep because I'm so nervous. I'm not afraid of crashing as much as I am hitting turbulence. It does bother me knowing we aren't on gravity. I am going to keep this short since I need some sleep. I just finished watching a horror movie with Allie and Kathleen. We were all screaming in Allie's room. I'll write more tomorrow.

Erin

JUNE, 2002 9:00 A.M.

After an hour delay on the runway because of a bad Storm, we finally took off. I was squeezing Allie's hand until she had no circulation left. Allie gave me the window seat because I wanted to watch everything from the window. Now we are in the air and above the clouds. I just turned to Allie and said, "This is what I've been afraid of all these years. This is nothing." Allie laughed and said, "What do you think I've been telling you for years?" I am going to enjoy the rest of the flight. My aunt will be waiting at the airport.

Erin

JUNE 2002 10:45 P.M.

I had a wonderful trip. We did so much in the nine days we spent with my aunt. Texas is a hot state. There is no way I could live there year round. We went to water parks, the mall, walked through million dollar homes, rented movies, swam in the pool, played cards, and so much more. I got so much sun. My aunt was also watching a little puppy while we were visiting. It was so playful and cute. I didn't want to say good-bye. I'm going out tonight with my sisters and friends into town. I'm living in Wisconsin all summer. Well, got to go take a shower.

Erin

JULY 2002 5:00 P.M.

While away in Texas I got the best sleep. I am still getting good sleep, but the flashbacks haven't stopped. They come when I least expect it. As much as I love summer I hate the fact that I have to see Brian all the time in Wisconsin. He is always at the beach with his guy friends or his girlfriend. His parents bought a place this past month in Wisconsin. They are down the street from us. So both of my houses are within walking distance of Brian's house. I feel no matter which way I turn I can't escape my past. I often find myself wondering if it will haunt me the rest of my life. I don't think I can live like that. Well the Fourth of July is tomorrow. We will be going to the Abby in Fontana like we do every year, but that doesn't stop me from seeing Brian. All my relatives will be there like every other year. Thankfully we don't sit with them. I look forward to the Fourth of July every year. The twenty minutes of fireworks in the sky over the water are so beautiful. I like the really big ones that remind me of willow trees. When we come home from the Abby, we do our own fireworks on the street in front of the house, which is exciting. Anyway, I'm going to go swimming at the beach with my cousin. I'll write more tomorrow night after the fireworks.

Erin

JULY 2002 12:45 P.M.

What a night it has been. We drove in the back of my neighbor's truck the whole way to the Abby. It was fun because we had to lie down so no police would see us. On the way home it was even worse because police were everywhere checking to make sure people weren't driving drunk. Every two seconds my dad and neighbor would say "Cops!" We would all lie down in the back giggling. At the Abby we ran into some boys who graduated with Brian from my high school. They realized who my mom was because she worked at the high school, so they put it together that Brian was our cousin. One of the boys turned to Allie and me and asked us if we knew what our cousin Brian was going to be doing tonight. Allie and I both said, "No" and we didn't care to know. The boy went on to say that Brian was sleeping over at the Abby with his girlfriend and was going to be having sex with her. Right after he said that Brian came walking towards us with his girlfriend. Immediately Allie and I turned around walking the opposite direction from Brian. I felt a flashback coming on bringing me back to the day Brian abused me in the bathroom. The flashbacks are so intense I sometimes have a hard time knowing if it is really happening or not. The rest of the night went smooth and I did the best to enjoy myself. I'm going to bed now.

Erin

JULY 2002 1:00 A.M.

I went to the racetrack near my house in Wisconsin tonight. I went with my mom, Allie, and Allie's friend Kathleen. We had a blast. I ran into my grandma today. I haven't spoken to her since her birthday last month. I have hurt over the years because of her and grandpa's response to

Brian's actions. I deal with a lot of anger that they have caused me. She can get on my case for saying the word "freakin," which she feels is swearing, but yet doesn't get on Brian's case when he molests his own cousins. Real fair, grandma, wouldn't you say? If she can't be fair and is going to protect Brian I don't want to have anything to do with her or grandpa. I don't need to be hurt again. They spend so much time supporting Brian and are rarely there for my sisters and me. What really upset me is grandma and grandpa went with Brian and this family to his college orientation (to visit his college.) They have never gone with any other grandkids, only Brian. Like Brian is special or something. It drives me crazy. The worst part is they came home wearing sweatshirts they bought with his college name on it. They wear the sweatshirts all the time. Walking around like proud grandparents. Gosh, I would be really proud knowing I have a sexual perpetrator grandson, too. Always protecting the underdog. I'm going to write my grandma another letter tomorrow. Anyway, if I talk about this anymore it is just going to make it harder to fall asleep. Good night!

Erin

LETTER TO GRANDMA 6:30 P.M.

Dear Grandma,

I guess after my last letter I didn't get my point across. We talked back in December and obviously you don't see what I see. I can understand it is hard to accept the fact that you have a grandson that committed a crime, but to be in denial about it and favor him makes me wonder why you would protect someone who did something so terrible to your grand-daughters. You've been supportive of Brian since you learned of the abuse. Have you ever once called me up and asked how I'm dealing with it? Have you ever shown me your support? If anything our relationship has been distant since you learned of the abuse. I've seen you show up at all Brian's football games, and I even learned that you and grandpa went and visited colleges with him. What bothers me so much is how many times I called you up and invited you to my bowling meets that were held inside, not outside in a stadium like football. Yet you never came to one of the meets I invited you to. You always made up an excuse. Do you realize why I didn't call you once during my sophomore year to come? I know you have anger towards my mom for contacting the police, but if you should be angry with anyone it should be Brian. Brian is the one who committed the crime. My mom was just taking care of her girls. What all mothers should do. You'll never be able to understand the pain I have gone through. You probably never saw my pain because you have been too busy cheering Brian on in life. I must live the rest of my life with the abuse I suffered as a child. I guess I don't understand you. I don't understand how you can get upset over a word I said and get on my case about it, but not say one word to Brian about the crime he committed. A crime people spend time in prison for. I don't want to lose the relationship I have with you, but I am not going to continue to put myself through this. Living around a family in denial. Pretending it never happened is the easy way out, but sooner or later the truth is going to come back to slap you in the face. The truth hurts. What can I say? When you are ready to accept the truth and quit favoring Brian, give me a call. This letter isn't meant to upset you. It is to open up your eyes to the truth you don't want to see.

Erin

JULY 2002 10:30 P.M.

I had a fun day and night. I spent the whole day at the beach sunbathing, swimming, and eating lunch. Tonight I played cards with Allie and mom. It is always fun when the three of us play cards together. Last night I had a new babysitting job. It was for a one year old named Lexie. She was such a good baby. After putting her to bed I watched the news to hear if there was any information about the nine trapped miners in Philadelphia. By midnight they were all confirmed alive. By two-thirty all were pulled from the mine alive. It is a good ending to a horrible experience. It gave me a good feeling inside to see all the families celebrating for their loved ones. Giving me a little hope that one day things will get better for me.

Erin

AUGUST 2002 10:45 P.M.

There is a terrible thunderstorm outside right now. I love a good storm. I'm the only one still awake. The longer I stay up the better chance I have of sleeping through the night. Last night I had a horrible dream of being trapped in an alley in the city at night and Brian was cornering me and then began attacking me. I woke up and began crying and couldn't stop. I lay in bed wondering how many more years must I continue to run from my past. Will it haunt me forever? I ask myself that often. What do I have to do to move on? Mrs. P told me throughout the school year that things would get better eventually. All I want to know is when. I am sick of running from my past and then having it come back to haunt me. I just want the answers to all my questions. I can only handle so much. I'm sick of constantly being caught up in the nightmares and flashbacks that I can't snap myself out of. I better end this here before I begin crying. I'm just sick of crying myself to sleep at night. I want someone to come take the pain away.

Erin

AUGUST 2002 4:30 P.M.

I don't know how to explain what I did yesterday. I guess I will begin by writing about my time at the beach. I was at the beach all day today with my sister Allie and a bunch of my cousins. We were all out at the raft-playing king of the raft. One after another we would push each other off into the water. I was so caught up in the game I didn't see Brian walking down the pier with his friend and brother. When I saw Brian dive off the diving board and swimming out towards the raft I felt a sudden panic come through me. My heart began to race and a flashback began. Images of that last night Brian abused me flashed through my head. The feelings of being trapped in my aunt's room were suddenly all coming back to me. As I saw Brian getting closer I immediately dove in the water and began swimming towards shore. Once on the beach again I grabbed my towel and sandals and began walking back up to the house. Out of nowhere I began crying and couldn't stop. Once I reached my house I went inside and a sudden terrible thought came over me. A thought of cutting myself to numb the pain I am feeling. I suddenly felt an urge to find something sharp. I remembered my mom had her sewing basket here. I found the basket in a closet and found a needle and quickly went across my wrists two times until I saw blood. It hurt, but I could handle the physical pain any day. The emotional pain is unbearable.

Now that I've found this new coping method, how will I hide it I wonder? I will tell my parents I have an ear infection so I can't swim. I did have one earlier this summer that prevented me from swimming. I'm being called for dinner. Dad made hamburgers on the grill.

Erin

AUGUST, 2002 4:30 P.M.

Grandma called me today. The phone was ringing and I happened to be the only one inside and picked it up. It was grandma and she was calling to talk to my dad. She asked if it was Erin and I told her it was. She went on to say she received my letter and said she doesn't understand why I feel that way. "I don't feel I favor Brian." I just don't get into it. "I treat you all the same and I am sorry if you think I favor him." I just was like, "Yea, yea, whatever, grandma." She then asked if we could make up and be fine with each other. I just said, "Fine." I just wanted to get off the phone with her. She honestly is in complete denial and doesn't want to accept the fact that her family is not perfect and she has a grandson that has a sick mind and needs major help. I finally got her to hang up, but before she did she said, "You aren't going to avoid me anymore, right?" I told her I wouldn't. I just needed to get off the phone with her. I guess getting all upset about this is only making it harder for me. I need to learn to accept that my grandparents are in denial and can't handle the truth. I am headed out the door to go baby-sit all night.

Erin

SEPTEMBER 2002 8:00 P.M.

I'm a junior in high school now. School started last week. Junior year is going to be a tough one. I have the ACT test to take in April and my grades mean the most this year. I am reading a poem I wrote over the school PA system during the announcements. I wrote about September 11th, this being the one-year anniversary. I like my schedule except for my last period. It isn't so much the algebra as it is the teacher. The teacher is so negative. I can't believe she can even have a teaching degree. The first day of school she doubts all her students. I don't have a good feeling about that class this year. I have continued to cut when having a flashback. It is the only way for me to snap out of the images running through my head of being abused. I've been wearing long sleeves to cover up the scars. I am ashamed of it, but don't know what else to do to let go of this pain that continues to haunt me.

Erin

SEPTEMBER 2002 9:40 P.M.

Hiding in the dark in a small walk in closet. The children are looking for me. I thought I was alone until I feel the cold hand of someone else. That someone else is my cousin Brian. He whispers in my ear, "Stay quiet." I know what is about to happen. I can't see a thing, only a little light coming from underneath the door. Brian wraps his legs around mine. He slowly slides his hands down my pants. I cringe! He slowly rubs me down there while breathing his hot air on my neck. I scream, the flashback is over with another cut on my arm.

Erin

OCTOBER, 2002 8:30 P.M.

Dear Mom and Dad,

I'm so sorry you must discover me this way. I don't want to cause you anymore pain then you already have, but my pain is too much for me to handle. I can't bear to face another day of flashbacks and nightmares of the abuse I suffered at the hands of my cousin. You both are incredible parents that always showed me your love. I in no way want either of you to blame yourself for my death. There was nothing you could do to stop me from taking it to this step. I was miserable and depressed and am now going to a much happier place. A place where this pain isn't felt and I will be free. None of this is your fault. You both have given me the best childhood. Something terrible happened to me and I can't live to see another day. I hope you don't look at me ending my life as a selfish act. I just can't handle the pain. Don't mourn for me instead celebrate that I am somewhere happy. I thank you both for loving me and being my parents. You're the greatest parents anyone could ask for. I'm in God's hands now where I am safe and free. This was for the best I promise! I'll be watching over you. I love both of you don't ever forget that! Love,

Erin

OCTOBER, 2002 11:15 P.M.

The pain goes too deep into my soul. I can't take it. I feel trapped in my own body. I don't know how to express my pain. I keep too much bottled up inside. I continue to run from my past and I feel it has caught up with me and I no longer want to live. I am taking my own life tonight after my parents turn out there light. I've struggled for too long and can't bear another day in this hell I live in. A hell I'm terrified to talk about. I want to go be with God where this pain does not exist to a place where I will be much happier and not so depressed. It saddens me it must end this way, but I can't bear another day. The scars expressed on my arms tell it all. I enter the bathroom and close the door, leaving a letter by my bedside for mom and dad in the morning where they will discover my lifeless body. Untwisting the cap of the bottle I read the bold word Tylenol. One by one I pop them in my mouth and swallow. After swallowing around twenty white pills, a sudden panic sets in. This is a sin I won't be forgiven. I'm making a huge mistake. I stick my finger down my throat and puke up the small white pills. Tears stream down my face. Sitting on the bathroom floor in tears like the night I came home after being abused trying to scrub away the dirty feelings. Eventually I climb in bed and cry myself to sleep.

Erin

OCTOBER 2002 7:30 P.M.

God was with me two nights ago when I tried taking my own life. I feel he is the one who put a stop to it. What surprised me is the very next day Caitlin asked me to go to church with her. We haven't gone in a long time. So I went with her and we had a great time. It felt so good to listen to Bill Hybels, the pastor, talk about God. The music was very uplifting and I began praying to God to forgive me for my mistake of trying to take my own life. I am just hurting and I feel God understands my pain.

Erin

OCTOBER 2002 10:00 P.M.

I made a promise to myself four years ago and followed through with it last month. I returned to the Children's Advocacy Center and I am becoming a volunteer. The same place I broke my silence and had my girls' group will now have me in return help them out. It is my way of saying thank you and showing my appreciation for all they do. I've started watching children while parents are in support groups. I will be doing this until January when I am given a new volunteer opportunity with the center. I am really enjoying it and feel it is one way I'm working through my pain by giving back. I also did some research and found a woman in Florida who runs an organization called SAFE which stands for Stuffed Animals For Emergencies. She was happy to ship over boxes of stuffed animals to the Advocacy Center for children after their interview. It had an impact on me when I had my interview giving me a feeling of comfort. I feel it is a great way to let the kids know everything is going to be ok. On top of that, I am also volunteering at a local nursing home. I go in every Tuesday and play ball with a group of seniors. I also manicure the ladies' nails, hand out mail, and help them get ready for supper. It is really a great learning experience that I feel will benefit me down the road.

Erin

OCTOBER, 2002 8:30 P.M.

I am on the school speech team and this is the speech I will be giving. Deer Crossing. Railroad Crossing. Stop for pedestrians in walk way. Do not pass-stopped school bus from either direction. These are all warning signs that can help protect you and your loved ones, but what happens about the warning signs that aren't posted . . . but should be. Don't talk to strangers. Look both ways. Or even, **WARN-ING!** Sex offender lives here!

It is estimated that 50-90% of all sex offenders repeat the same crime. Their victims are innocent and unable to defend themselves and are also unable to understand the depth and severity of the crime being committed against them until it is too late.

Recently in our history, a law, known as Megan's Law, was passed, allowing citizens the right to know if a sex offender lived in their community. While this law helps identify potential danger, much more should be done. What about the people who don't know about the law or have access to the records? What about the children who may not understand exactly what it means? Society needs to do something more than just post names and addresses. The most wanted criminals are posted in the post office . . . Why not sex offenders? One judge in Texas has decided that serious crimes deserve serious consequences. As a result, changes have been made so that everyone has the opportunity to know where sex offenders live and if they are anywhere near them. The first thing this judge did was to require all convicted sex offenders to post a sign on their home stating, "Sex Offender Lives Here." Neighbors, parents, and children are clearly able to see the sign and watch for danger. The second item was a bumper sticker. It is placed on the offender's car so that anyone seeing it can watch for indications of cruising, or looking for the next victim. These are enforcements that happen in one small town in Texas. The rest of the country should stand up for this right, the right to know where danger lurks. In addition to knowing this, states should also require a "home arrest" type of tracking system. Though this may be costly to manufacture and track, but the benefits definitely outweigh the money . . . your children will be safer. The laws are not tough enough in many states. It is important that America stand up for the right to have safe neighborhoods and to be able to keep children out of harm's way. We have drug education, car and train safety training, seatbelt laws, curfew laws . . . but no laws that help keep convicted offenders identified and tracked. Therefore my commitment to America's future is to protect the lives of innocent children from becoming victims of child molesters. If every state began to look seriously at easy ways to protect our young, many children would not be potential victims. They will be saved from humiliating, degrading, and life-altering events. They will have the opportunity that I did not have as a child . . . for I am a victim.

Erin

OCTOBER 2002 9:25 P.M.

I'm still cutting, which is really bad, but it is the only way I have found to work for me. I went in this week to the school psychologist. Miss P. isn't at the school anymore. The new psychologist is Mrs. Ardell. She seems like a very caring lady. My friend Sarah convinced me to go in and talk to her. I made an appointment and saw her this week. I don't know when I will feel ready to talk about the past. For some reason it is very hard for me to open up. I spent the time talking about school with her. I am going to continue to see her once a week. Allie introduced me to her last year because Allie knew her from our junior high where she worked right after I left. Hopefully with time I will be able to open up to her. It is going to be hard talking about this all over again like I did with Miss P. I did see Miss P. at a football game last

weekend. She is always so happy. Anyway I have to take
Chance for a walk before bed.

Erin

NOVEMBER 2002 10:45 P.M.

Tonight I went to church with Caitlin. We have been
going every weekend, but tonight the message was particu-
larly good. The pastor talked about problems in families and
forgiveness. It had a big impact on me listening and relating
with it. The pastor asked if we would be the outcast this
Thanksgiving. It was like he was describing our family
dynamic. I am always the outcast, keeping to myself the
entire night. I also went to the high school football game
with Sarah. We won by one-point. After the game Sarah and
I drove around the neighborhood and I told her I needed to
tell her something. She pulled up in a parking lot near my
house where we sat in the car talking. I eventually got talking about how things have been tough and then I told her
about my self-injury behavior. She asked to see my wrists
and told me I need to get help. I told her I don't know what
to do, but it is the only thing that works for me.

We talked for a long time and she promised not to tell anyone, but also urged me to tell my mom or someone I trust. I
also went to my Aunt Jenny's house this weekend. I came to
see her new baby boy again. She had him October 19th, the
same day as his dad's birthday. So father and son are born on
the same day. I think that is so cute. I'm babysitting next
month for her. It will be fun to be watching the little baby.
They named him Christian and he'll go by Chris. I had a
pretty busy weekend. I am tired so I will be ending this here.

Erin

NOVEMBER 2002 6:30 P.M.

I saw Mrs. Ardell today. I still have not yet told her any-thing about my past. I pretty much keep the conversation on school. Speaking of school, I am failing Algebra two. The teacher doesn't know how to teach and I do terrible in math. I think I will be dropping it and taking it again next year with a new teacher. I am so stressed out for the holidays. I dread them every year for the same reason. Having to sit at the same table as my abuser and the meaning of the holiday is being thankful. I've decided this year that if I can't take it I will just remove myself from the table. I need to remember to breathe.

Erin

THANKSGIVING DAY 2002 11:30 P.M.

The evening was going okay until I ran into Brian when he was entering the kitchen and I was leaving. I immediately began to panic and had to keep reminding myself that I am no danger. It wasn't helping and the memories began to build which caused me to go in a back bedroom and pull myself together. Instead I cut. When it was time to eat I took as little as possible and was finished within a couple minutes. Grandma had only taken one bite of her meal by the time I was done. I went in the back bedroom and played on the computer. I feel I can't be myself and I'm always on guard when Brian is around. Even though I know he can't hurt me, just the sight of him scares me. All the relatives think it was just something minor. They have no idea how badly Brian abused me. They will learn the truth one day.

I'm lying in bed thinking of the last four years. The rest of the family is sleeping and I am asking myself a bunch of questions I can't answer. I'm going to turn out the light and go to sleep.

Erin

DECEMBER 2002 11:15 P.M.

I am babysitting tonight at a hotel in the city for my aunt and uncle. Allie is with me, but she is already asleep. Both the three-year-old twins are asleep and the new baby is asleep right next to me. I've been sitting here thinking about something. I remember reading in a book about sexual abuse survivors. It says that people's sense of smell can often bring up flashbacks reminding them of how things smelled at the time of the abuse. Well, since I was born without a sense of smell, shouldn't I have less flashbacks than I do? It doesn't make sense. I still think the reason I have my dog Chance is because God had something to do with it. Chance has a terrible smell that comes from his skin because of infections in his ears. Everyone stays away from him, except me. I can't smell him at all. I still think it has to do with the fact that he sleeps in a cage. I would love to let him start sleeping in my room. I do get many comments about how pretty Chance is. I love him and don't know what I would do without him. He is a great dog other than the fact that he wants to eat every minute. My aunt and uncle won't be back for a couple more hours. The view from our window is unbelievable. The city is amazing at night. Oh, the baby is beginning to wake up. Later,

Erin

DECEMBER 2002 10:50 P.M.

I had an awesome day! School went well and then after school I had my holiday choir concert at Indian Lakes. We arrived at school at four-thirty. Yesterday mom almost discovered my wrists. She was helping me find something nice to wear underneath my robe. I kept trying to tell her I would be fine doing it on my own so she wouldn't see my arms. I kept trying to delay her. She found a skirt for me and I told her I could handle finding a top to wear. This is the third time in three months she has come close to finding out. I feel like I am walking on eggshells trying to hide the truth. The dinner was good and singing went excellent. I really got to know some people that I had never spoken to. One guy named Jeremy sat next to me and I had him laughing all night. He is a very quiet boy who doesn't say much. At the end of the night we surrounded the tables and sang to the people. Jeremy didn't know the words to the song and I had him laughing the whole way through it. I am very exhausted now so I think I will end this here. Night!

Erin

DECEMBER 2002 3:45 A.M.

Another nightmare has me up. I was on the couch hiding under blankets. My heart was pounding and I could hear Brian coming. Suddenly I feel his hands on my legs. I scream and wake up and feel my own heart pounding like I'd just run a marathon. I now can't fall back asleep. I continue to toss and turn. I never fall back asleep and get up to the sound of my alarm clock.

Erin

DECEMBER 2002 9:45 P.M.

At church tonight the Pastor asked us what we want for Christmas. Not in the meaning of presents. He gave us the example of peace. The pastor then let us sit in silence and think. I began creating the best Christmas gift. A gift where the flashbacks would end, the nightmares would go away, the self-injury will be in the past and not present and I will be happy, not depressed. I just want to stop crying inside for my lost soul. I just want happiness.

Erin

DECEMBER 2002 10:00 P.M.

Pain

Tears stream down my face
I feel like I am in a race.
I want to curl up in a ball
And make a final call.
Asking Daddy to take me there
Where life will be fair.
I would not feel this pain
Or see the rain.
My soul hurts like a stinging bee
And all I want is to be free.
I close each eye
And just want to die.
I cut more each day
As the sky turns gray.
Someday I'll see the sun
When will that day come?
Until then I close my eyes good night
For another dreadful fight.

December 2002 11:00 p.m.

I received a thank you letter from the Advocacy Center for getting them in touch with the lady who sent over the stuffed animals. Tonight I wrapped presents at the Advocacy Center until ten thirty. I helped out a lot. I feel good about what I was doing. I had a great time with the ladies who work there and some other volunteers. I also saw Cathy while I was there. She gave me a big hug, but was in a rush out the door to leave. I will see her Thursday at the Christmas party I am helping at. I am very tired and need some sleep. Night!

Erin

December 2002 9:00 p.m.

It is a week until Christmas. I am excited and nervous. Excited because my family is going to Florida and it will be my first time there. I'm nervous because I must face two days of my cousin Brian. First at Christmas Eve and then Christmas day. I had another flashback yesterday. The flashback didn't surprise me, but it was when I had the flashback, during gym class. I buried my head in my sweatshirt and kept it there until the memories stopped coming the memories of his breathing, his rising chest against mine, and those hands. I can see it and feel it all so well. If only I could chop those hands off. Anger eats away at me when these memories appear again and again, always somewhere dark and quiet.

Erin

December 2002 9:40 p.m.

I went to the city yesterday with my sister Caitlin and Allie. We went with our church group from Willow Creek. We were painting the inside of a building, in a poor and rough neighborhood. It was nice to meet new people. My sisters and I were putting paint on each other's clothes. I didn't get home until six. I then had to go baby-sit for my Aunt Jenny and I ended up spending the night because she didn't get home with my uncle until two a.m. Well, I am really tired and need some sleep. I have school tomorrow.

Erin

Healing

"The weak can never forgive.
Forgiveness is the attribute of the strong."

—Mahatma Gandhi

JANUARY 2003 8:00 P.M.

Christmas was difficult like usual, but I managed to make it through Christmas Eve and day. Christmas Eve we all put presents under the tree for people we had to buy for. Well Brian had to buy for one of my younger cousins and instead of wrapping it in Christmas paper he wrapped in newspaper. It gets worse though, it wasn't just any newspaper. It was the obituaries. Now is that sick or what! What a freak! Just thinking about it gives me the chills.

It was nice to go to Florida and see the Ocean for the first time. The drive was really long, but once we got there it was beautiful. The first night Allie and I went walking around outside the condo. It was much different than Illinois. There are no palm trees in Illinois. We spent a day at the ocean. It was beautiful. The sand was so soft on my feet. We had food with us and we began feeding the seagulls and then we had tons of them surrounding us. I tossed a pretzel on the hat my mom was wearing and a seagull came down, sat on mom's hat and ate it. Mom screamed of course and then we all began doing it to each other. Right before we left for Florida mom was discussing things we should bring on our trip. She reached down and lifted up my arms and asked what all the scars were from. I told her the cat did it and she immediately accused me of cutting myself, which I found suspicious. She dropped it and we didn't discuss it any more until this week. I learned that mom read a letter Sarah wrote me about my self-injury and that is how mom knew.

Today was the day mom found out for real what was going on. Sarah went to Mrs. Ardell and told her about my self-injury. When it came time for lunch, Sarah said she wanted to show me something and began walking me towards Mrs. Ardell's office. Right before we got there Sarah informed me that Mrs. Ardell was waiting for us. I tried turning around, but Sarah insisted that I get this over with. We walked into Mrs. Ardell's office and sat down. For the next hour Mrs. Ardell asked me what was going on that would cause me to do this to myself. I began telling her about the abuse and how it's taking over my life. I told her how it was difficult to talk to mom about everything. I explained the flashbacks and nightmares I have. She informed me that either I need to talk to mom or she is going to sit down with her. I told her I couldn't, so she planned to talk to her tomorrow and wanted me to come halfway through the period to meet with them in her office. She told me that I needed to get outside help for this. I held back the tears. Mrs. Ardell told me things would get better I just have to give it time. I had a hard time falling asleep last night dreading today. Mom was called in fifth hour. I came halfway through the period and Mrs. Ardell opened the door. Mom sat there looking very unhappy. Mrs. Ardell asked me if there was something I wanted to tell mom. Staring at the table I mumbled, "She already knows." Mom jumped in and said, "Erin I don't understand why you are doing this to yourself. I thought everything was going good for you. Does this still have to do with the Brian thing?" Mom went on to say, "I try to make your life good and be there for you. Why are doing this?"

With that I began crying and told mom that she always wants to put the blame on herself like she is a terrible mom. I didn't know what to say to make her understand my pain. Instead I put my head on the table and began crying. While I cried Mrs. Ardell and my mom talked about getting me outside help. Mom eventually had to leave which left just Mrs. Ardell and me in the room. Mrs. Ardell tried to calmly get me to talk to her, but all I wanted to do was cry. Cry for the pain I couldn't get rid of. The pain Brian is to blame for. Mrs. Ardell eventually got me to stop crying and take some deep breaths. She told me, "your mom agrees you need help and wants to help you." She gave my mom the names of some therapists for me to call. Mrs. Ardell told me we would talk again Monday to see how the weekend went. I thanked her for her time and headed off to my history class. It is nice to have someone like Mrs. Ardell to have available. When I got home that afternoon from school, mom was not happy. She was upset and hurt that I did not come to her about the self-injury. She later talked to my dad that evening about the situation. She gave me the list of the therapists and told me when I made an appointment to get her insurance card from her. I called the first lady on the list who was highly recommended. Her name was Dr. Stern. I left a message on her machine and she called me back tonight. We set up my first appointment three weeks from now because her schedule is full. I hope I can learn to open up and let go of this pain. I hope this is the answer I've been waiting for.

Erin

FEBRUARY 2003 9:40 P.M.

I turned eighteen on Groundhog Day. It was a nice birthday. I went out to dinner with the family and opened presents. My childhood years are gone and I'm left with the memories. Growing up as a child playing with Barbie's, baby dolls, having slumber parties, lemonade stands, and playing school. My childhood didn't end when I turned eighteen. My childhood ended when Brian took my innocence. A childhood that can't be replaced.

Erin

FEBRUARY 2003 5:00 P.M.

I had my first appointment today with my therapist. Her name is Debbie and she seems very nice. Today I filled her in on my painful past with Brian. I told her how the family has been divided ever since it happened and the heartache it is for me with the flashbacks and nightmares. Just when our session was up she asked me if I was harming myself in any way. I informed her of the cutting and she asked to see my wrists. She told me we would work on it. I am almost afraid to open this door of pain that has been closed for so long. Pain I don't want to let others hear. My next session is next Thursday at four.

Erin

FEBRUARY 2003 10:35 P.M.

The Storm I'm Stuck In

When I hear the rain
It reminds me of my pain

Like the thousands of tears
I've held on to all these years.
Then I see the lightning
Which can be frightening.
Just like my dreams
When all I hear are my screams!
Eventually comes the thunder
Reminding me of being under.
The covers pulled over my head
On the very large bed.
The flashbacks give me the chills
Reminding me I can end it with a bottle of pills
I look up to the sky
Wanting to cry.
The stars shine bright
But in my dreams there is no light.
I lay and watch the time
Paying for his crime.
I see the sun begin to rise
As tears fall from my eyes.

Erin

FEBRUARY 2003 6:30 P.M.

Dr. Stern, my therapist, explained to me how I am experiencing symptoms of PTSD, which means Post Traumatic Stress Disorder. She explained it and it made sense. PTSD is very common in men that have gone to war. Many sexual assault survivors experience it. I told her about my suicidal thoughts and attempt. We talked a lot about my self-injury. She told me she wants me to get to her two H's, which are healthy and helpful. She told me I was doing something helpful, but not healthy. She ended by asking me to come up with a list of things to do during a crisis situation when having a flashback or urge to cut. I'm going to go get started on that now.

Erin

MARCH 2003 8:55 P.M.

My Past

Look back on my past
Seemed to go by too fast.
Except when I was being held down
And told not to make a sound.
Trying to hide my tears
But he saw my fear.
Holding me down on his bed
Having to do what he said.
Taking me under a sheet
And feeling his sweaty feet.
Not knowing what to say
As he began to play.
Every time seemed to be the same
He acted like he was in some game.
Only hearing the sound of his breath
Made me think of death.
Trapping me in his house
Was like a game of cat and mouse.
Closing the doors so no one could see.
As I struggled to be free.
After two long years I ended the game
But life after that was never the same.
That is all for today.
Maybe tomorrow I'll have more to say.

March 2003 2:57 a.m.

I'm awake from a terrible dream. I was locked in this house I'm unfamiliar with. There is no way out. The windows are barred up and the doors locked from the outside. I'm not alone. Brian is coming towards me to make a move. I run to the basement where he follows me down. It is dark and gloomy. He catches up and shoves me on the couch, using his hands to rip off my shirt. As he lies on top of me I wake up. It is 2:57 a.m. I can't go back to sleep. I will wait till I hear the sound of my alarm at 5:30.

Erin

March, 2003 7:30 p.m.

I was going through a box of photos tonight when I came across a picture of my grandparents' condo in Wisconsin. Above the door is the number 269. The memory hits me. The night so crystal clear it was like it happened yesterday. Waking in the middle of the night with Brian's hands down my pants as he is fingering me. I immediately panic, grab his sweaty hand and put it on his chest. Looking over at him he gives me a cold stare. The flashback ends.

Erin

March, 2003 10:30 a.m.

I can hear his faint whispers in my ear telling me to stay quiet. I use my hand trying to push his weight off me, but he is powerful and I grow weak. He's using his hands to feel my chest. Then taking my hand and forcing me to feel his penis. Rubbing my hand up and down it. I make a fist trying not to feel it. He begins kissing me. I beg him to let me be. Another flashback, another cut, another day scared and alone.

Erin

MARCH, 2003 8:30 P.M.

We made it to Colorado after driving from 7:30 in the morning until 10:30 at night. We stayed at a hotel where the parking lot was filled with snow. The next morning our car was dead. A man was nice enough to get it started up again with jumper cables. When we got to our condo at the resort we got settled and Allie and I went to find the pool. We spent the evening playing cards and watching television. Today we skied all day. It was beautiful. The mountains are amazing. Sitting on the chair lifts with the sun hitting my face. I always feel the closest to God here remembering last year when I was on these mountains. It is unbelievable what God has created. No matter what though, wherever I go, the memories come with me. While coming up a chair lift, I had a flashback. It was a short one, but it frustrated me. It is like I can never escape them. I had a flashback in Florida while looking at my reflection in the ocean, and now I am having flashbacks on the chair lifts hundreds of feet off the ground. I just want to enjoy my vacation. I am going to make the best of it. Good night!

Erin

MARCH, 2003 3:15 A.M.

Another nightmare has me up. I was in a city all by myself and could only hear the sounds of cars from a distance. I am walking past tall sky scrapers and see no one in sight. I suddenly feel like I am being followed and continue to look over my back. I start to pick up speed and see a corner I can turn at. Just as I turn the corner I run right into a man. I scream and take off running, turning down different streets. I suddenly make a horrible mistake and turn down a dead-end alley. Looking back, I see the man turn in and he corners me against the brick building of the alley. Near a dumpster he beings stripping me of my clothes. I wake up in pouring sweat terrified. I've been up for about an hour analyzing the dream. My interpretation of the dream goes back to the night Brian came home and chased me around his house until I was stuck upstairs, just like in the alley in the dream. Eventually being locked in a room and abused. There was no one in the city except passing cars on the nearby highway and the night I was abused there was no one around except the passing cars on the street outside. It makes perfect sense. I wonder often if Brian ever laid in bed at night feeling horrible for what he did. Someday when I get the courage I want to confront Brian. I have nothing to be afraid of and I am not weak anymore. I should not fear him.

Erin

APRIL, 2003 9:30 P.M.

It has been five years this month since I broke my silence. Yet it still feels like it was just yesterday I was being held down and told not to make a sound. The memories are so fresh. I often wonder how my life would have been different if I had not been abused. I feel I wouldn't have the determination that I do now. I feel I wouldn't have the passion to help others the way I do now. In fact there was an article in the paper last month about my volunteer work. It was a nice article. Every night I lay staring at my ceiling wondering how other victims of abuse cope with life. I feel like I will live in this pain forever. My therapist has been very helpful in making me understand my feelings and open up. She has made it clear that I should not be blaming myself that I am not at fault for what Brian did to me. I recently had a flashback in her office and she helped me through it. Dr. Stern has worked with me on relaxation skills. She is also teaching me how to ground myself when I am being triggered with a memory. Once a week I sit in her office staring out the window on the tenth floor at the parking lot of the mall below and watching the cars pass on the highway. Too afraid to show my tears, I look the other way. Dr. Stern mentions that I should try writing a letter to Brian, but said I don't have to send it. I told her I have done that before, more then once. She feels it will be a good way to help me let go of some of the hurt I'm feeling. I often wonder what Brian has been thinking the past five years. She told me I could write a letter to Brian and then burn it. She said that could be therapeutic for me. I might give it a try.

Erin

APRIL, 2003 7:15 P.M.

I talked to Mrs. Ardell today. She asked if I am still self-injuring. I couldn't lie and told her I was. We talked a lot about my sleep pattern. I get very little sleep an average of three or four hours a night, which makes it harder in school for me. Every week when I see Dr. Stern, she asks to see my arms. This past week she was shocked to see how much I cut myself. Mrs. Ardell started working with me on a book about people that self-injure. Every time I come in she has a page marked to read to me. She also has me filling out a daily task sheet on my self-injury and how I felt before and after. Mrs. Ardell and Dr. Stern see my determination to get better. It is having people like them in my life that give me the strength to move forward each day.

Erin

APRIL, 2003 12:30 A.M.

I've been doing a lot of thinking lately. Everything from my past is fresh in my mind. It has been years, yet it still feels like just yesterday that I was begging him not to rape me. I had a lot of mixed feelings tonight sitting in my room wanting to cut and end the images flashing in my head yet the same time knowing it will just cause me more pain and cause me to think about taking it a step farther. I guess the only thing that keeps me from taking it that step farther is holding out faith that someday it will get better. Yet looking back it has been a lifetime of pain. From my childhood up into my teen years and now following me into my early adulthood, the same painful pattern. I can't even escape the pain in my sleep. It chases me wherever I go. I know people look at me as this "downer" person and it bothers me. I wish I didn't look like that person. I walk with my head staring at the floor in school. I try my best to pretend life is great and hide my true feelings, but it isn't always that easy. Especially when they are all coming out at once. I stand in front of my mirror every now and then and look at myself. I see my soul crying inside. My soul has two doors attached to it. When I open these doors I see shelves like in a closet with millions of memories stacked on top of each other. Entering my soul I begin coughing. Dust is piling on top of memories too

painful to talk about. Instead of dealing with them, I close
the door and let the memories collect dust. I tried turning on
the light to my soul but the light does not work. For my soul
is a really dark place. A place that has been kept stored with
painful abuse too scary to express. I hope with time I will be
able to dust my shelves and clear out some of the pain piling up in my soul and make room for happier things. Maybe
then it won't be so dark. I'll be able to turn on the light. For
years I have kept those doors closed not letting anyone in.
Hiding the truth. It relates to when I cut, which is my way
of expressing my pain and not letting anyone in on the truth.
Just like with the doors to my soul I use my sleeves to cover
my wrists. If it isn't a fake smile hiding my dark soul, then it
is long-sleeved shirts hiding my scars. I sit back and wait and
wonder when the light will come on, the true smile will
show, and the sleeves will be rolled up. "When?" I ask myself.
Someday soon, I hope.

Erin

APRIL, 2003 2:00 A.M.

An incredible step I took tonight. Where do I begin? How
do I explain this to you? You're going to be so proud of me.
I've never been prouder. I went to my youth group where we
had a scavenger hunt. It was so much fun. The night was
going great. When I came home I was triggered with a flashback. I began to walk upstairs towards my bedroom to get my
razor and begin cutting. When suddenly stopped myself and
turned around. It was like something tapped me on the
shoulder and made me turn around. I went back downstairs
and got on the computer. I went online and looked up an old
"forward" my grandma sent me. This same "forward" she also

sent Brian. I copied Brian's e-mail address down and began typing a letter. For the first time in five years I am confronting my cousin through this letter. When I finally finished a little after one in the morning I sat staring at the computer screen, too scared to hit send. Reading it over and over again I finally hit send at 1:45 A.M. My adrenaline is going. I can't believe I did it. There is no way he would respond to it. I put so much of my anger into the letter. Letting him know how much he hurt me. He probably won't even open it and will just click delete. I wouldn't be surprised, but guess what? I took the step and confronted him through a letter. Here is what my letter said. It isn't friendly at all!

Brian,

This letter is probably coming as a complete surprise to you, but I didn't feel I should warn you since you never warned me when you were going to use my body for your own damn pleasures. When I look at you I see nothing but scum. I don't know how you live with yourself after the crime you committed over and over again.

You're probably wondering why I haven't forgiven you since you did say you were sorry. Well maybe if you meant it, I could try forgiving you, but soon after the night you apologized, I learned from a friend that you had assaulted her while she was under the influence of alcohol. The sad thing is it wasn't the last time I heard you had done this to a girl. Last year while at school I learned yet again that you tried raping a girl at a party. Hearing this just makes me sick and I soon realized that when you apologized you didn't mean it. You were asked to apologize by someone in the family that I respect just so we would go to Grandpa's 70th surprise party.

Brian let me turn the tables and put you in my place. Do you know what an effect your actions have had on my life? You have left a permanent scar on my life that can never be erased. It has been years, but I still wake up at night with nightmares running from you. I still have flashbacks of you lying on top of me or slipping your hands down my pants. It seemed any time I tried to escape you, somehow or another I would fall back in your trap. The memories are all so fresh as if it happened yesterday. You even had the nerve to do it to me on your bed while your brothers played Nintendo. How sick can you get? You made my holidays a living hell not knowing if I was going to be able to escape the sick thoughts running through your mind. I'll never forget being at Uncle John and Aunt Debbie's for Christmas Eve and you locked me upstairs with only a night light on. You just sat there by the door staring at me. My heart was racing a hundred miles an hour terrified at what you might do. Looking out the window I began to pray to God you would leave me alone. A twelve-year-old should be opening presents and singing Christmas songs, not praying to God that her cousin wouldn't lay a hand on her. I think that was the only time you were ever interrupted when you had me trapped. That Christmas God heard my prayers when John knocked at the door and interrupted whatever you were about to do. That didn't stop you, though. You just had to get your hands on me. Sure enough later that evening you did. How evil can you be?

Brian, I stayed silent for so long giving you so much control over my body. Having you brainwash me for two years into thinking no one would believe me. Do you know how many memories I have stored in my head of being somewhere with your hands all over me? I can still remember the first time it happened as you slept next to me in

Grandpa and Grandma's condo. I woke to your sweaty hand down my pants fondling my crotch. Waking up to that I remember pulling your sweaty hand out and looking over at you with your eyes wide open and then you pretend to be asleep. I may have been young, but I am no dummy. You were fully aware of your actions. Brian, how about the time in the crawl space in your basement under the blankets as David was upstairs counting for "hide and go seek?" You laid on top of me slipping your hands up and down me and then putting your mouth on mine and breathing your air into my mouth. Brian, I don't forget something like this. This is something that will stay with me the rest of my life. I can remember every detail as if it happened yesterday. I will never forget the horror of going in your parents' walk-in closet and sitting down not knowing you were in there and you sat there quiet as possible and then made your move by wrapping your legs around mine, you began to fondle me and all you could say is "Shh stay quiet," as your brother and my sister were looking for us. I can still hear the sound of your breathing and it makes me want to VOMIT! This is just a small portion of the memories I have stored in my memory bank of falling in your sick trap.

What really pisses me off, Brian, is I listened to you and stayed silent not telling anyone about what you were doing to me, and behind my back you began doing it to Allie too. HOW DARE YOU! I get angry just thinking about it. How fucking dirty can you get? I remember being so terrified when I would see you come home while I baby-sat your brothers knowing what you had in mind. Did you ever think once about the hell you were putting me through?

Do you know what it has been like for me to walk down the halls in school as a freshman and see you? It was like living the nightmare all over again. What is even worse is to attend a football game and hear your name being shouted by Mr. Berns after you ran a touchdown. Every game I went to I prayed you would lose. I'll never forget at the pep rally last year when Mr. Berns stood you up in front of everyone and called you a hero to our school. OH, SOME HERO, BRIAN! LETS JUST STAND UP AND CHEER YOU ON! Oh, how I wished I had stood up in front of everyone and told the crowd what a fucking asshole you are. I don't think if you looked up "hero" in the dictionary you would find "cousin who sticks his hands up and down his younger cousins' pants." How about when that guest speaker came to our school right before prom to talk about drugs, drinking, and sexual assault? Towards the end of the assembly the man asked the student council president, class president, and football captain all to come on the gym floor and look around and see everyone standing who had been a victim of drugs, drinking, or a sexual assault. The last I heard you were Football Captain, so why weren't you out on that gym floor looking at everyone standing up? Maybe because you knew Erin and Allie and maybe even someone else would be standing up in that crowd because of your actions. Was someone feeling a little GUILTY?!

Lets talk about the holidays. Do you actually think I enjoy being there? Well, of course I do when you aren't around, otherwise I would rather change smelly diapers or clean toilets then spend a holiday with you. Thanksgiving you are supposed to be thankful. When we bow our heads at Thanksgiving with you sitting across from me, all I can be thankful for is when we leave and I don't have to be in the same house, let alone the same dinner table, with you. After all you abused me in Grandma and Grandpa's garage on Thanksgiving one year. Great way to celebrate! As you probably have already seen, at holidays I can't *stand being in the same room as you. I always have to get up and leave because I can only think sick thoughts when I see you. You are a symbol to me that represents pain, anger, fear, control, evil, and power. I still feel the pain, anger, and evil towards you, but I am no longer afraid and I am the one with all the power now. In fact at Easter this year when I was given the opportunity to hit that piñata, I took all my anger from over the years I've had towards you and put it all into that piñata. As you could tell I was determined to beat the shit out of it! I would have been really happy if I missed the piñata and actually took you out. Maybe next Easter! You go about life like it is great and for you it probably is. You never had to suffer like I have over the years. You took away my innocence, my childhood, and my ability to trust others.*

What really pisses me off is the fact that your mother fought with the State Attorney because she didn't want you to have a record because then you wouldn't be able to play football. Well, she did a damn good job of fighting it and you didn't get punished at all for the hell you put my family and me through. Well, you may feel you got off easy and you're right, you did. But I just look at it this way, if you think you are going to meet your maker someday, I would think again! I go to church. I know where creeps like you go after they die. Then you can truly experience suffering and understand what I have been dealing with all these years. I do a lot of praying. I don't pray for you, but I pray for the innocent children you might father someday and hope they don't fall victim to your sick fucked up mind! I look at the word "hate" as a really strong word. You're the only person in my life that I will always hate. I never want to see another person fall victim at your hands. Maybe someday you will be able to get restored and get help before you find yourself behind bars.

I've been running for years fearing you when the abuse was going on and now in my dreams I do the same. I no longer run and hide from you though. Instead I turn around and get in your fucking face letting you know I am not afraid of you like I was in years past. Just when I am about to turn around, I beat the shit out of you. I've thrown you off cliffs, tied you to trees, fed you to the bears, and tied you in a large black garbage bag and watched you suffocate. Oh, I almost forgot; I've cut off that dick of yours, too.

We were a close family that did everything together before I told our secret. Your actions took it all away and you will always be to blame. You are at fault for making all the holidays uncomfortable and the entire family will never look at you the same. The family may stay in denial forever and never want to learn the truth, but, Brian, you and I both know the truth, the truth that follows you every day. Yes, you may have taken my innocence, but you have not taken my strength and courage and, to be quiet honest, I would hate to live the rest of my life with your past. I didn't hurt anyone like you hurt me. Your past will hang over your head the rest of your life. I am going to share a poem with you I wrote a year ago about how I feel towards you.

Lost Innocence

I once loved you
and trusted you too
until one fateful day
you took it all away.
the touch of your hands
was only one of a mans'
your weight was too strong

you know what you did was wrong.
I wake up in the night
to your awful sight.
I sometimes look to the sky
and wonder why?
I've asked God plenty of times
why you committed these crimes.
I remember watching the clock
as you pulled off your sock.
Taking me under a sheet
Feeling your sweaty feet.
I wanted to run and hide
as you looked on in pride.
you pushed me on to carpeted floors
behind closed doors
not knowing what to say
as you begin to play.
you put your hands all over my chest
Wanting me to sit back and rest
as you slid your hands down me
I struggle to be free
wishing I could spit in your face
as my heart continues to race.
you tell me not to tell
just as I am about to yell.
my body goes numb
looking at you evil scum.
the night is over, but it didn't end there
of course you didn't care.
this went on for years
which brings tears.
In the morning sunrise
I dry the tears from my eyes

Someday I'll get my way.
Just watch
YOU'LL PAY!

The last line says it best. Someday I will get my way. You will PAY. I don't know when, but when you do I will throw a party and celebrate. The nice thing for me is I made it through the abuse and survived and I no longer have to worry. What sucks for you is yours is still coming and you don't know when!

The time it took you to read this letter would be considered seconds compared to the time you spent forcing you're hands all over me. My only advice to you is to find a church and start praying because from my viewpoint the way you're headed is straight to hell. I'll be curious as to how they treat men who are screwed up like you in hell. Maybe chop you up and throw you in a fire and watch you burn. After all, that is why they call it burning in hell!

As you can see, Brian, I have a lot of anger built up and I have every right to say what is on my mind. You can't even imagine the hell you have put me through. Words can't describe it. I am not looking for an apology because right now in my life I won't be able to except it. I want to someday be able to forgive you, but you would have to be able to show me you got the help you never got before and when that time has come you will know. Then maybe you will be able to come to me on your own when the time is right and apologize, but right now in my life I am not ready to forgive you. I only know you as the cousin I once trusted, loved, and cared for who took away my trust, childhood, and most of all innocence. I know you for who you were back when you had control over me and used your power to abuse my body. What you did can't be erased. Even if I were to ever forgive you, it is something that has left a permanent scar on my life forever, a very painful mark.

You don't know how difficult it was for me to finally put all my feelings together from over the years and write you. I did this all on my own and no one, not even my parents, knows I have contacted you. I hope you can answer so many of my unanswered questions such as what made you do this to me? Why Brian, did you hurt me like this? Did you ever feel guilty when you did this? It seems as though the abuse got worse as time went on. Why did you lie and say none of it happened after I broke my silence and you were confronted? You actually were going to try and say you did none of that. Did someone abuse you that made you do this to me? Do you still have the urge to do this to other girls? Over the past years have you ever once laid in bed wonder what you put Allie and me through? Did you ever try writing an apology letter? I might even be wrong and you still have had sick fantasies over the years of me. Brian, the least you could do after all you have put me through is explain to me all these unanswered questions. Like I said, I am not looking for an apology because I am not at a point in my life where I can forgive you. I am not even close to forgiving you as you can probably already tell by the anger I have in this letter. I have all the rights in the world to be angry and maybe the truth is, I will never be able to forgive you.

I would appreciate a response to my novel e-mail that has been weighing on my heart for such a long time! I am only looking for the truth, Brian! Nothing but the truth!

Ex-cousin
Erin

May, 2003 7:00 p.m.

I can't believe it. I never would have imagined Brian responding to my letter. I opened my mail this morning to see his name in my inbox of e-mails. I was too afraid to open it and my adrenaline was running wild. When I got home Caitlin was there. She came home for the night from Wisconsin. I was so glad to see her. She asked me to go out to get something to eat with her. While at dinner I let her read my letter to Brian. She went on to say she would never expect him to respond. I looked to her and said, "He did." She was shocked. I told her that I hadn't read it yet. She immediately insisted that we go home and read it together. We quickly finished dinner and headed for home. As we both sat at the computer, I finally opened the e-mail. This is what it said.

Erin

I know I messed up as a teenager, but God has given me another chance in life and I am making the best of it. I live my life in the best way I know how. I wished what happened never happened and that I could erase it all, but now I accept what I did and I am going to keep on looking to the future and keeping the past as a reminder of my mistakes in life. I don't know what else you want me to say, but that is all I will say.

Brian

It didn't say much, but just the fact that he responded surprises me. I am now working on what I will respond back with.

Erin

MAY, 2003 8:00 P.M.

For the past month Brian and I have been dialoging. Immediately after the first letter I sent, I went to see Mrs. Ardell the next morning. I was out of breath and she knew something was up. I told her over and over, "I did it. I sent the letter." She was shocked and was so impressed with me. I gave her a copy to read and headed off for first hour. I then saw Dr. Stern and she could tell by the look on my face something was up. I started off by saying, "I wrote a letter to Brian like you asked, but not only did I do that, I sent it." She couldn't believe it. I then sat there in her office reading it to her. She complimented me on my writing skills and asked me if I thought he would respond. I told her I never expected a response, but received one.

Now I am preparing for the upcoming wedding. My uncle is finally getting married for the first time. The wedding is taking place in Wisconsin. I don't think anything will be different. I still see him the same way, only I confronted him for the first time since I broke my silence. My cousin Sarah who just came back into our lives will be coming also. She is my Uncle John's daughter. He didn't know about her until she was eight-years-old. They never formed a relationship and she just came back into our lives again. She is unsure of her father and mainly wants a relationship with some of her cousins. My uncle John has been taking her out to try starting a relationship, but so far it is pretty rocky start.

Right after the wedding is our last week of school. We have finals and then it is summer. I can't wait to be a senior in high school! I'm almost out of the house and on my own!

Erin

MAY, 2003, 6:00 P.M.

Brian,

Now that we have broken this barrier I have so many unanswered questions, thoughts, it is like my mind is spinning. I've been hurting for so long I just don't know what to say. I guess the least you can do is start by explaining to me why you did what you did. I guess what I find myself wondering is if you were abused and that made you act out on your own abuse as a teen. Brian, you may be able to look to the future, but I am struggling to make sense of everything that happened when I was a child. Trying to make sense of all the flashbacks that occur and nightmares that keep me up at night. You say you wish you could erase it, but the truth is we can't. Brian, I am finally opening up and talking about all the abuse that I held in for so long. A part of healing myself is confronting you and having to hear what you have to say. I am sick of living life with a bunch of secrets. The abuse was a secret and the entire family acts all secretive about what happened. Brian, no matter what, you will somehow have to be a part of my life because you are family and we will always come in contact some way or another. I don't want to live the rest of my life having so much anger and hate towards you like I do now. I am sick of living life in fear and pain. I take each day one step at a time. This week I took one huge step in e-mailing you. My email was a very angry one and it is how I feel. Someday down the road I want to be able to send you a letter where I no longer feel the anger and hate that I feel now, but instead be able to let the past go and forgive you. It isn't going to be easy either. I want there to be a day when I don't walk past you in Wisconsin or at a family party without getting the chills and feeling sick. Instead

*being able to say "Hi" and maybe even have a conversa-
tion. But I can't do this on my own and, now that I have
contacted you, you have to be able to work with me.
Starting off by answering my questions. Right now I am in
a very angry stage of life because of your actions. I hope you
can help me better understand why you did what you did,
and if you were abused, and what you have been thinking
over the years about all of this. Brian, have you ever gotten
yourself some help? You see, that is my biggest problem. For
me being able to forgive you, I have to know that you have
been restored and gotten the help you needed. In some
ways I think you're afraid to go into what happened in the
past. You can admit to it, but the question is, can you get
the help you never got? I always wondered when the day
would come that I would contact you. You probably wonder what made me contact you. Well, I had another flashback of the past on Wednesday night and, Brian, I don't
know if you know exactly what a flashback is like for me.
But to give you an example, it is like being put back in a
room with you putting your hands all over me. I can feel it
all over again. So I am constantly feeling violated like it is
happening all over again when these flashbacks occur. So I
finally decided it was time to vent my anger towards you
and let you know how much pain you caused me. So now
I ask you to start to tell me what you think, and have been
thinking all this time since I have opened up so much about
the past to you. This is a starting point for me and I hope
you don't back away now, because then nothing will ever
come of this and I will continue to feel anger and hate. I
look at it this way: I stayed silent for so long for you while
you continued to abuse me. The least you can do is explain
yourself to me and answer my questions. I will not judge
you and, like I said before, this is staying between us*

because it isn't anybody else's business. I just feel you were holding back from saying a lot to me because you are afraid I will get angry. Well, you have to understand, I do have a lot of anger, but that is just one of my ways of venting. So say what is on your mind. I'm listening! I am giving you this opportunity to explain yourself and ask for forgiveness. You can pass it up or keep in contact. The choice is yours!

Erin

MAY, 2003 9: 45 P.M.

Erin,

I asked for your forgiveness a long time ago, but I can see it wasn't accepted and with rightful cause. I got help a long time ago if you didn't know and I am living life the best way I know how. I never meant to hurt you the way I did and I don't know why I did what I did but I am honestly sorry for it. I also know I have destroyed our family and that kills me every day, too. I don't know what more you want to know but honestly that is how I feel. I am truly sorry for any pain and suffering I have caused you and our entire family.

Brian

MAY, 2003 9:30 A.M.

Brian,

I do have to say I was shocked to even hear any response from you to begin with. I really didn't think I would hear back from you. You have to understand this isn't going to be easy for me. For five years I have held in all the memories of the abuse. It was just this past year that every-thing came pouring out and I have begun to work through it all. I am taking each day one step at a time and it is going to be a long process for me to work through. I am going through a lot of different stages and feelings in my life trying to work through this all. As you can tell by my first letter, I am in a very angry stage right now and that is just part of me working through it all. I hear what you have to say, Brian. You are saying you're sorry. I hear that. But right now I have just begun to open the doors and start working through what happened when I was a child. I can also understand your mother's pain. She has suffered a lot over the years, too. I would hate to be in her shoes to hear that her son did this and not know what to do. I am taking baby steps to work through this. Right now I still know you as the per-son you were back when the abuse was going on and you had all the control because that was the last I ever had con-tact with you. I would love to jump right to it and tell you I forgive you, but it isn't that easy. I am working through it all and I came to a point in my life where I needed to contact you, which was a HUGE step for me. My healing process will continue and sometime down the road I will get to the finish line and be able to come face to face with you and say I forgive you and let go of the past. I'm just starting to walk down this painful road in life and I would love to jump right to the finish line and forgot all the crap in between, but it just isn't possible. It may be a year or two starting point and I've let you know how I feel. Hopefully you can look forward to the day when I can forgive. I will look forward to that day, too. The day when I no longer live with so much anger and hate that I'm feeling towards you. The day I know that you really are a changed person and no longer that monster I've known you as all these years. At least you know that I am taking the steps to get there. It is going to be difficult to see you after knowing I have contacted you about all of this. The least I can ask you to do now is pray. Pray for my soul to heal, pray for the day when I am no longer angry and hate you, pray for the day when I can FORGIVE YOU!

Erin

MAY, 2003 1:30 P.M.

Erin,

Trust me, I was more shocked to get an email from you than you getting a response from me. Besides that, I hope and pray every day that one day you can forgive me and I know that it will take time, but I wish you the best when walking down that road and I hope that it will lead you to your well-being in life and forgiveness of my sins.

Brian

MAY, 2003 7:30 P.M.

Well, Brian, a week ago I never imagined I would be contacting you. In fact my plans were to never have contact with you again. Started seeing a therapist a couple months ago trying to work through all these years of pain I've held in and never discussed. The problem I have had in therapy is getting into the abuse and talking about the details and working through it. I have come to the conclusion that I am afraid. I am afraid because it is like I have been a prisoner in my own body for so long because I still feel the control you had. When I would try talking about it, the fear and control would come over me and I would close up and numb myself. So in the past few months I began to realize if I am ever going to move on and heal myself the first step I have to take is to confront you. The problem was I've been scared to death to send a letter to you. I have stacks of letters that I have written to you that I just never sent, but it was my way of venting. I've realized neither my parents, sisters, friends, therapist, nor even myself could break this chain of fear and control that has been hanging over me for so long. It had to be you. I realized I am getting nowhere. It has to be you to take that control and fear you had on me for so long and let me know it's all right, let me know you no longer can hurt me the way you did before let me know I can begin to heal my soul and work through everything. Then I can break out of this prison I have been in and work through it all and get to the finish line. It took me five years to realize it has to be you to free me since it was you who locked me up so many years ago. Because you are the one I'm afraid of and you are the only one who can take away that fear. So let me know that I can stop being afraid of you and tell me you no longer are in control. I need to hear it from you. Brian, I know how you feel about being shocked when I sent that e-mail to you. I sat in school the whole next day and couldn't focus because a million thoughts were running through my head. After all it wasn't a pretty e-mail, but I think I couldn't have explained it any better to get my point across. You see, not only do I mourn for what happened, I mourn for the relationship I lost with your family. Think about it, Brian, we grew up doing everything together and the years before the abuse happened were some of the best. So I feel the sense of loss too. I know I have taken a huge weight off your shoulders that probably follows you every day by letting you know I am giving you a chance. I want to see the light at the end of the tunnel when this is all through. I want you to be held accountable for your actions. I want you to quit living in denial and accept what you did. The extremely ill feelings I have towards you seem impossible to get rid of. I just need to be able to break free of this prison that I have been living inside of that was caused by your actions.

Erin

MAY, 2003 12:00 P.M.

Erin,

If venting all your anger towards me in your letters is the best way to help your therapeutic process, then do it. I am here to listen to what you have to say. I don't know how you want me to release you from this prison, but I assure you that I have changed for the better in life and will always be the most humane person I can be. Are you looking for evidence of me being a changed person and then you will be released? Because if that is it, then all I will do is try to convince you that I have changed my life.

Brian

MAY, 2003 5:50 P.M.

Brian,

I can't begin to tell you how weird this all is for me right now. To be honest I feel like I am in a daze or a dream and haven't woken up yet. This just all doesn't feel real to me that I'm actually talking to you and letting you know all the pain and anger I have and you are actually responding back. What is going to be even harder is when it comes time for me to see you face to face at the next family holiday or up in Wisconsin or in the neighborhood. I've gotten so used to knowing you will be there and I've been used to acting as if we are complete strangers. The next time I see you and times after it will be so much different. I can't put on that stranger act because we are now communicating each other. No one else in the family will see the difference, because they don't know that we are talking, but for me it will be difficult because there is no longer this wall that I used to have between us.

This road I am going down in my life right now came to a complete stop and I couldn't move on. It was like there was a wall I would run right into and couldn't move forward. That wall has been there for five years and I haven't been able to get over it until this week. This week that wall came crashing down and now I am ready to begin to heal and start walking down this road. Now that I have overcome this HUGE accomplishment of contacting you I am taking you as a passenger down this road and you are coming with me ever step of the way. I was a passenger down your road for two years before I escaped. Well, I am the one locking the doors today and taking control of the wheel as I take you down this painful journey with me to healing. You are going to feel every single bump in the road we hit the same way I do. You are going to travel through the storms with me and when we finally get to the end of this road, if you haven't already bailed on me and convinced me that you are a changed person, I will turn the engine off, step out into the sunshine, take in some fresh air, and forgive you of your sins. So fasten your seat belt because I am the one who has the control now and we have a LONG journey ahead of us.

Erin

May, 2003 8:00 P.M.

Brian,

Your mother stopped me after school one day and asked if I could watch David and Jake while she went grocery shopping. You weren't home and I began playing "hide and go seek" with the boys. After a few times of playing you came from the garage and saw that David was counting and you turned to me and said you had the perfect spot to hide. You told me to follow you and so I did. I didn't think twice about it. It had been such a long time since the incident in the condo that it didn't even cross my mind. I followed you down in the basement and you took me into the storage area/crawl space and took blankets and told me to hide under them. So I did, thinking nothing of it, and thought it would be even harder for David to find me. I could hear David above us upstairs running round looking for us. You made your way under the blankets and began touching me. Running your hands under my shirt and then leaning over and putting your mouth on mine all I can hear you saying my name over and over again in a soft whisper. I begin to tell you I'm going to go upstairs, but you refuse. Eventually we hear David make his way to the basement and open the door to the storage area. You tell me to stay silent. Oh, how I wish I had screamed. Instead I closed my eyes trying to imagine being somewhere else. Once we hear your brother make his way back upstairs, you pull the blankets over our heads and get on top of me. You now are forcing your hands down my pants and you begin to fondle me. My heart is racing and I am trying to catch my breath. Your weight is too strong and I see nothing but the darkness around me and feel the touch of your hands all over my body. You begin to move your body up and down in a humping manner. I am scared and so confused at what is taking place and don't know how to make sense of it all. I try to go away in my head pretending it isn't happening. The abuse continues until we hear the sound of your mother's high heels on the tile floor above us as she walks in the door. You immediately get off me and make your way to the door. You make your way upstairs and I follow a few minutes later. Very shaken up, I try to hide it in front of your mom. Your brother David gave up looking for us a long time ago and now he sits watching TV and asks where we have been all this time. I go home that day and once again hold in the truth. This day that this took place in the storage area, did you plan it? It seemed like you saw the opportunity to get your hands on me and jumped right into the game we were playing just to make me fall in your trap.

Did it give you some kind of rush of excitement? Another thing that has been on my heart for a very long time is Molly. You see, Brian, she lived with you for 6 or 8 months. I have wondered for years if you ever laid a hand on her. I look at all the warning signs. She won't spend the night at other people's houses. I feel that she saw what happened to the family and didn't want to cause any more pain and anger so she stayed silent and still hasn't worked through what happened to her. I am not accusing you. I am just asking you a simple question.

Erin

MAY, 2003 3:30 P.M.

Here it is. These are my opinions and my side of the things that happened. I don't recall that happening in the basement. What I remember is helping you hide but I never once fondled you down there. The only abuse I ever put you *through was in Wisconsin and I admitted that and I accepted my mistake and got help for it. Yea, I may have been close with you and Allie growing up and playing games with you guys, but never once did I abuse either of you like I abused you in Wisconsin. That is what I remember. Those are my memories of the events that happened.*

Brian

MAY, 2003 8:30 P.M.

WHAT! I don't know what to say. Listen to yourself, Brian. Can we say Denial? If you are going to try to tell me that is the only memory you have then you are in denial. I can't believe you can even say that. My anger is boiling that you could make a comment like that. You must have buried a lot of memories. You're a perpetrator and you know it. That fact that you can say it only happened once makes me wonder how sick and fucked up you really are. No matter what you have to say, in my eyes, once a perpetrator always a perpetrator. So if you are trying to tell me that it only happened in Wisconsin, then explain this. Explain all these other times you abused me! What about the time in your parents' walk-in closet, on your bed while your brothers played Nintendo, on your green bean bag chair that was in your bedroom, in the basement while we played blanket monster, in your parents' bathroom, in grandpa and grandma's garage, in your parents' bedroom when you came home that night while I was babysitting, in your closet....I could go on and on. It just angers me that you are going to try to say it only happened once. What a bunch of shit! With Allie you abused her in the basement, and in your parents' bathroom. I am trying to give you a chance and hear you out, but if you can't admit to it, then there is no point in this discussion and we can go on living the life we have been living for the past five years and you will never be forgiven. It is up to you. I lived through it I remember ever damn detail like it were yesterday. You know damn well what happened. You're too afraid to admit to it because you don't have control or my silence anymore. It may be easy for you to forget, but not for me! I just can't get over the fact that you are going to try and tell me you never did any of this besides the first time it. happened. I get sick just hearing you say that! You denied the abuse back when we came out about it and now you are going to try and tell me you never did any of this to me. The first step you have to take is admitting to it. I would in no means make up a bunch of bullshit. Obviously I have these memories for a reason and obviously you are in denial about the truth or are too afraid to go there because there is too much guilt. That is sad! Really Sad!

Erin

MAY, 2003 10:30 P.M.

Erin,

All this happened in the past and that is where I wish it could stay. Think of a person you like and respect and now think if you found out that they did the things I did. That is how I feel about my past. I look at my past as if I was a different person and I don't want to know anything about him. I don't want to be me at times. That is one of the worst things that someone can say about one's self in life. At least you know you are a good person, Erin. I want to be a good person so bad, but every time I feel I am, I look to my past and I realize I can't change my past and who I was and I will never be a good person. Sometimes the best way to live a good life is to forget about my past for a while. Bringing this all back is ripping me apart and you're probably happy for that, but no matter what you do or say to me, it will not help me look back at my past and forget who I was. Because remembering who I was helps me to be the best I can be today and in the future. I don't know how going through all these details will help you to get over what I did to you, but maybe you can explain that to me and I could help you more. I don't know. But that is what I have to say.

Brian

MAY, 2003 10:30 P.M.

Brian,

I have wondered what has been going on in your life over the past five years. There have been so many nights I lay staring at the wall wondering if you have changed your life. Wondering what has been going through your head. It is very confusing to me because I know you as the person that hurt me and not the person you are telling me you are. Yet you have made the effort and are continuing to respond and that makes me feel that you are trying. Even though I know some things I say you don't want to hear because it disturbs you. I'd like to know how you got help back when this all came out. Because what disturbs me, and you may admit to this or you may not, is the fact that I did learn over the past five years that you had tried to do this to other girls. I heard it happened in Wisconsin to one of the girls up there and maybe it did and maybe you can admit to it and regret it. I also heard on the bus last year that you tried to do something to another girl at a party. See, that is

where I get concerned. Even though this is none of my busi-
ness, it will help me understand that you can honestly
admit to your mistakes and that your hormones got the
best of you. I am not here to judge you, Brian; I am here to
learn how you have changed your life and how you can
admit to your mistakes. Last week when you tried to tell
me it only happened once, I got so angry. I wasn't even
going to respond, but I realized that would get me nowhere
and that we both knew the truth It was just a matter of
getting you to admit to it. I want to know the steps you took
to change your life over the past five years. Brian, I believe
everyone is born a good person. I once knew you as that
good person before anything happened. I believe evil got in
the way and made you act out, which has caused so much
pain and anger over the years. I want there to be a day
when I am not filled with so much anger and hate. I really
thought I would live the rest of my life with this pain, anger,
fear, and hate hanging over me. I never thought it would
come to me confronting you and you actually responding
back. I want to know what you are thinking and have been
thinking over the years and I want the truth. Even though
it sounds as though I have been spending all my time hurt-
ing, I have also done a lot of good for others over the years.
I want to hear about you first though. Then once we get
through the past, maybe we can look to the future.

Erin

JUNE, 2003 7:45 P.M.

Brian,

Just as long as I get an answer. It is going to be hearing
what you have to say in response that will make me

understand who you are. Brian, even though you have no memory of ever being abused yourself, in my heart, I feel something happened to you when you were young.

Someone who abuses someone else usually is acting out on something someone did to him or her. You may have no memory of it because it happened when you were just a child. You may have dissociated the memory, or it may be something that has been weighing on your heart for many years. You see, right after before the abuse came out, when my mom was on the phone with yours, your mom mentioned that you and Mike had a babysitter once that drew naked pictures while babysitting you. Now that is a little strange and who knows what else happened. You say you are going to answer my questions but want to feel comfortable first. I think you're afraid to trust me. I am not going to push you into answering my questions, but when I get to the end of this road, if you expect me to forgive you, I am going to need answers. Like I said in a pervious email, I think eventually it is going to have to be that we come face to face and discuss this. I think once we do that, It will give me a better understanding of who you really are and it will let you know that I am trying to understand you. Maybe once that happens you can open up and express more to me, because when it gets down to it, I am going to want the truth about everything. I think also if we have the opportunity to talk in person, it will end these flashbacks I constantly have. Let me know what you think.

Erin

JUNE, 2003 8:30 P.M.

Erin,

Five years ago I promised many people that I would not talk to you one on one, face to face, just us, me and you alone together. Each person that I promised had certain reasons they gave me and I respect each one. And I understood each one. Maybe someday I can talk to you face to face alone, but right now I am not comfortable with that.

Brian

JUNE, 2003 8:30 P.M.

Brian,

I am not comfortable with it either right now. I am just saying someday it is going to have to happen for me to be able to forgive you because I want to hear it from you that you are sorry. I am sure you were told by many people not to communicate with Allie or me because it could get you in trouble. Well, that is still the case with Allie because she is a minor. I am an adult now and can make my own decisions. One of those decisions is to eventually have a talk with you face to face. To hear it come from you that you are sorry and want forgiveness and you have changed your life. When you are ready, Brian, let me know, because I think it will take a huge weight off my shoulders knowing I can actually hear it from you and it will get us one step closer to forgiveness and I know it won't be easy.

Brian, as much anger and hate as I have had over the years towards you, I don't want to see you suffer the rest of your life with guilt and shame. I have suffered too many years and don't want to suffer any more. I want you not only to be able to ask me for forgiveness, but to be able to forgive yourself, too. You have beaten yourself up over the years. At least we can go on living our lives the best way we know how and you can be at peace with your past and I can be at peace with mine. So I will put it this way, when you are ready and you will know in your heart that you are, come find me and ask for forgiveness on your own. I will look forward to that day and I am sure you will, too.

Erin

June, 2003 7:45 p.m.

Brian,

I came to a point where I needed to confront you. I took you along to let you hear the pain you caused me. I could question you the rest of my life and still not be able to make sense of why you abused me. There will be questions I may never get answers to, but in my heart I already know the truth, the truth that follows you every day and the guilt and shame that will hang over you the rest of your life. I'm learning to rebuild my life. I'm an adult now, but in a sense I am still that lost twelve-year-old hurting inside. I'm taking baby steps every day to relearn what you stole from me. My innocence can never be replaced. Every step I take forward I look at it as one step closer to closure on my past. You took away my ability to trust others. You took away many valuable years of mine that can never be replaced. I've been living my life running, fearing, and fighting you off. It's been five years since you laid a hand on me, but I am still trying to scrub away the dirty feelings I feel inside from you. I look forward to the day when I can feel clean and whole again and be able to free my soul of this dark world I have been living in. I look forward to the day when I can start on a new road in life that will be filled with happiness and will look to the future and not the past. The day when I can come to the end of this road I am on now. Then I will be able to start on a new road in life, which will involve a career, husband, and children. I will make sure to give my children the childhood that you stole from me. I can't erase the past so instead I am going to take my own experience and educate others. You took away my voice when I was young for so many years giving you the control to do what you did. You hear my voice loud and clear today and I plan to let the world hear me through my words some day. If that is shouting from the worlds' tallest building or writing am book, I'll be heard! I am no longer that fragile, innocent child you took advantage of. I am a woman with a lot of strength that is going to go far in life and heal others because of it. I am letting you know now that I am going to continue down this road by myself. You've heard the pain and anger you put me through, which you needed to hear. If you are honestly sorry, Brian, and want forgiveness it is going to take you coming to me on your own and admitting not to one, but to every single time you abused me. I would suggest getting outside help, because I feel you have been in denial with yourself about the abuse. You have dissociated with your past because you have too much guilt. It starts with you accepting the fact that you made some terrible mistakes and not being in denial about it. That is the first step you must take. The next step I see you having to take is turning to God and admitting to your mistakes and asking for forgiveness. Then you can take the next step and come find me and apologize for your actions and ask for forgiveness. If I truly see your remorse, I will find it in my heart to forgive you. Then maybe you can take the final step and look at yourself in the mirror and forgive yourself. I told you what I wanted you to hear, now it is your turn to act on it. I can easily go on living the rest of my life without forgiving you. I've done it the past five years. The question is, Brian, can you? I only want to hear it if you can really mean it. You will know in your heart when you are ready for forgiveness. You know the steps you have to take and I know the steps I am taking in my life. We are on two different roads in our life. I'm going to continue moving forward and hopefully some day we will cross paths and you will stop me and look me straight in the eyes and apologize and ask for forgiveness. It may be a week, month, year, ten years, it may be when I am old and blind, or it may never happen. The choice is yours. Do what your heart tells you. I would appreciate if you at least let me know you if you're going to try to take these steps or if you are going to go on living the life you have been living.

Erin

JUNE, 2003 11:15 P.M.

Summer vacation finally begins. I am spending my entire summer in Wisconsin like I did last year. The wedding was last weekend. It was a beautiful day for a wedding. I saw Brian for the first time in the church. I took one look at him and looked the other way. I still get sick to my stomach every time I see him. Which brings me to another situation. I need to come up with another way to deal with the flashbacks. We were also shocked this past weekend when Brian's mom invited us to their house for Mike's graduation party. I haven't been inside their house since the last time I babysat five years ago when Brian abused me. I am nervous to go, afraid it might trigger me. With the warm weather I can't hide the scars and stopped cutting a week before the wedding. I've tried stopping before and the longest I've gone is two weeks before I relapsed. Anyway I am going to give it another try. I am still seeing Dr. Stern weekly on Mondays. I am also keeping in contact with Mrs. Ardell over the summer through e-mail.

Erin

JUNE, 2003 10:00 P.M.

We went to the graduation party. There were a lot of people there. It was so weird walking in their house for the first time in years. The kitchen is all remodeled. I mainly stayed outside on the patio or in the kitchen with my sisters. I was holding my baby cousin while my other cousin was calling for me from the basement. I debated whether to walk downstairs. It had been years since I had been down there to a place that reminded me of the abuse. I pushed myself and made my way downstairs. I stood at the bottom of the stairs and didn't move. David and Jake have grown up a lot since the last time I was at their house. Jake is now in fourth grade and David is in seventh. The boys along with other cousins sat on the couch playing Nintendo. It immediately reminded me of the days when I used to baby-sit and was abused while the boys sat on the floor in the same room and played Nintendo. The same couch the boys were sitting on in the basement was the same couch I buried my head in while Brian abused me. Going down the stairs was a way of facing my past, which I felt I needed to do. Soon after I went back upstairs and saw Brian coming in the house. I immediately made my way for the back porch again. I eventually decided to walk home and take in the day. The entire walk home reminded me of so many childhood memories when I would walk home from Brian's house. The entire day was a big accomplishment for me, but it wasn't easy.

Erin

JUNE, 2003 7:45 P.M.

My uncle John is such a jerk. He told his daughter Sarah, who is my cousin that we blew the Brian situation into something bigger then it really was. It was no big deal he told her. He went on to tell her I need to get over it, and that Brian was just a hormonal boy. My cousin Sarah, isn't siding with him. She is siding with us and believes it was more then a little something that happened. She doesn't even consider my Uncle John her father. Her mother is engaged and she feels her mother's boyfriend has been more of a father then John. I totally agree with her. Well I wrote my uncle a letter. I don't take shit from anyone in this family.

Uncle John,

This is your niece Erin. I've been biting my tongue all week from saying something to you. I felt it best to wait after the wedding to say this since I didn't want to cause any problems before the wedding.

Sarah called me earlier this week and informed me on the phone about a few comments you said. John when I hung up the phone with Sarah my stomach was in knots and my anger was boiling. How dare you tell Sarah I need to get over what Brian did to me. How dare you sit there and tell Sarah what Brian did was a big nothing and he was just a hormonal boy. John you need to get your facts straight before opening your mouth and saying what you did. If you are going to tell Sarah what Brian did was a big nothing and call yourself a police officer on top of it, then there is something terribly wrong with this picture.

John explain to me how Brian locking me in Aunt Mary and Uncle Scott's bedroom and trying to rape me is normal. Explain Brian sticking his hands down my pants while I slept to be normal. If you call that normal then you are just as sick as Brian. John so let me turn the tables here. If this was your daughter that Brian did this to would you get over it, would this still be normal. What Brian did to me went on for two years and I had no control over what he did. You don't know the fight I put up for two years trying to get him off me and to leave me alone. You don't know the night-mares and flashbacks that have kept me up over the night for the past five years. You don't know the pain and anger that has been brought to me. Brian stole my innocence and ability to trust others. What makes things a hell lot worse is when I have relatives that protect him like Brian is the vic-tim. I am sick and tired of this family pretending and being in denial about what Brian did and blowing it off like it was a big nothing. Because John it wasn't no big nothing, yet you all want to believe it was and I've had it. This family including your parents want to hide the truth and pretend it never happened because after all, you all think you are the perfect family.

John I know about you calling the Schaumburg police detective handling our case five years ago when this all came out trying to protect Brian. Trying to get him off. Just because you're a cop doesn't give you any authority to change laws. I can't believe you had the nerve to do that. Did you ever here about the e-mail Uncle Mike sent my

mother saying what we did to the Brian's family stinks
and was totally uncalled for and we are never welcomed in
his home again? John think about that for a moment what
we did to Brian's family that stinks. What about what
Brian did to Allie and I. What we did to Brian's family
was try to get there son help because we didn't want him
to find himself in jail someday. Yet, we stink and Brian is
this saint that we should all rally around and cheer on.
John I am no dumb ass. I know how every single person in
the family except Aunt Jenny and Uncle Kevin and how
they feel about my family. You all pretend to like us, but the
truth is you all can't stand us. Well, if you care to know
how I feel about majority of the family is sick and disgust.

The entire family is in denial about the painful truth.
Everyone wants to hide by pushing it under the rug and
pretending it never happened and go about putting on this
fake act like we are one big happy family. Well John I've
had it. After the comment you made, after uncle Mike's e-
mail years ago, After going to hundreds of high school foot-
ball games and watching my grandparents' cheer Brian
on, After watching my grandparents' walk around in
Brian's college sweatshirts so proud of there grandson
Brian, and I am sure there is plenty more I haven't heard
that is being said behind my families back.

John I have many people in my life that care about me and
support me unlike you and majority of the rest of the family.
You all can go on pretending and being in denial about the
truth. To be honest I would have walked away from this
family a long time ago, but the only thing holding me back is
there are a few family members and cousins including your
children that I do respect and love unlike you. I don't feel I
should lose out on them because of something Brian did to me.

John I'll get over it when I am ready to get over it. Brian left a mark on my life that can't be erased. John a little bit of advice before I end this letter get your facts straight before commenting.

John, I will continue to pray for this dysfunctional family that is living in denial and hope one day you'll all be able to except the truth. It may not be until you read my book someday. Yes I did say book, I have a publisher waiting to publish my story of the abuse I went through. Someday the whole world will get to read the real truth behind this family. The truth behind many families. I'm not afraid to tell my story. Maybe then you will be able to learn what really happened behind closed doors for so many years at so many different family holidays. You can continue to support Brian and tell anyone you want including your daughter what he did was a big nothing. I lived through it, I was there, you weren't and I am the only one with the truth.

Believe what you want John, say what you want. I know the truth I lived through it!

Erin

Dear Erin,

I received your e-mail and I read your e-mail. To begin with I feel you need to get some counseling to get over your anger. It is too bad that this bad event in your life is foremost in your mind all the time. I was saddened by your comments, so many misinformed and immature. It's too bad that you have a yardstick out constantly measuring people and your extended family. It has never been nor should it ever be you and your family vs. everyone else. ENOUGH SAID!

Your loving Uncle John

I have no comment to what my Uncle responded back. All it will do is make me angry and I don't need to get worked up again.

Erin

JUNE, 2003 4:15 P.M.

I am working at the country club in Wisconsin with both my sisters. I am a waitress with Caitlin. Allie isn't old enough so she busses tables. I make good money doing it, but I can't stand our headwaiter, Mike. Actually no one can. He is a total loser. On top of that, we have a cook that is a creep. He flirts with all the girls. You don't want to get on his bad side. Other then that I am babysitting on the weekends. I am putting all my money in the bank for college. I've also been busy at the advocacy center watching two Spanish-speaking children who know very little English. It is very hard to communicate with them, but over the past eight weeks I've realized a smile goes a long way. I take the children to the park behind the Advocacy Center. I enjoy watching the kids.

Fourth of July is next weekend. We are going to the Abby resort like we do every year. It should be fun. There is always an awesome fireworks display. Anyway I am working tonight, so I must go wash my clothes.

Erin

JULY, 2003 8:30 P.M.

I don't understand Brian. He did something on the Fourth of July that totally shocked me. Like usual my family spends it with friends, while all my relatives go together. We are all at the same place, but in different locations. I was sitting on a blanket waiting for the fireworks to begin while my parents chatted away with friends. The rest of the kids were sitting on the boat in front of us. The fireworks started to go off just as Brian and his girlfriend came walking towards my location. He walked up on the grass about ten feet in front of me and sat down with his girlfriend. I was disgusted! I could not believe he had the nerve to do that. I immediately got up, walked towards mom, and told her there was no way I will be sitting here with him in front of us. I walked past Brian and his girlfriend and got on the boat. I was so angry that the one holiday I look forward to (because I don't have to spend it with Brian) and he comes and sits his ass in front of me. When the fireworks were all over I just wanted to go home while all the parents kept talking. My parents gave me the keys and Allie drove all the other kids and me home while the parents stayed to hang out. When I got home I went straight to bed. When I woke in the morning my parents were discussing how rude Brian was for having the nerve to sit down in front of us like that. I didn't go to the beach at all the next day knowing Brian was up. I baby-sat later that night for a one-year-old boy in a hotel. did the same thing the following night. The parents were going to a concert two nights in a row. Monday I had an appointment with Dr. Stern and told her how angry I was bout the Fourth of July. She couldn't understand why Brian would do that. I told her about some of my recent flashbacks and each one just makes Dr. Stern sick to know how manipulating Brian was. She checked in to see if I had been cutting and I informed her that I was staying away from it. Anyway I'm going into town with my sisters and friends for the night.

Erin

JULY, 2003 10:15 P.M.

I drove back to Illinois today because I had an appointment with Dr. Stern. We had a good session and we talked about relaxation skills. After leaving her office I left for home. On the way home I passed some children in a driveway holding up a sign that read "Lemonade Stand." It brought back happy memories of being a child and having lemonade stands in front of the house. I turned around and bought a glass of lemonade. Instead of handing them a quarter for the lemonade, I handed them a five-dollar bill. The smiles across the three children's faces as I handed them the money was worth every penny. I got back to Wisconsin just as the sun went down.

Erin

AUGUST, 2003 9:15 P.M.

Besides seeing Dr. Stern once a week, I have also been seeing Dr. Paul, my psychiatrist. She has me on anti-depressants, sleep medication and also anxiety medicine that I take only when needed. I usually take that before going to a family party where Brian is going to be. Right now I am at the beach. It is a beautiful day. I don't think there is a cloud in the sky. I often find myself wondering what my life will be like in ten years. I hold on to my dreams of getting my master's in social work and being a mom. I wait for the day when I won't feel like I am constantly living in the past. I want to hold on to the good memories, but I often find myself caught up in the abuse that has taken so much from me. The annual picnic is this weekend at my beach. Brian will be there like every other year. I just feel I can never be myself when he is around. I feel trapped inside. I am very proud of myself for all the progress

I have made since January. I have accomplished a lot. My biggest accomplishment will come in October when I do the Chicago Marathon for the Children's Advocacy Center. I have raised over seven hundred dollars by getting people to sponsor me. Getting people to sponsor me is the easy part. Doing the marathon will be the challenge. Well, I am going for a night swim at the lake with Allie.

AUGUST, 2003 10:45 P.M.

I didn't have to work today so I took the wave runner out on the lake. I had so much fun. I went as fast as I could make it go. I feel so free while riding it. I can go on it for hours. I love hitting the big waves. When Allie and I were younger, Caitlin would spin the wave runner in circles until we flew into the water. It is loads of fun! Allie has been busy spending time with her best friend Jennie all summer. The two of them together are pretty interesting. I am falling asleep writing this. Good Night!

Erin

AUGUST, 2003 6:30 P.M.

Today was the annual picnic down at the beach. I didn't see Brian until I walked out to the end of the pier and saw him at the raft. His girlfriend was on the pier with her friends and she began talking to me. She asked me how high school has been and I talked to her about college. When it was time to eat, we had a table right by Brian and all his friends. I did my best to keep myself together, but it wasn't easy. Brian was there a long time. After he ate he went back swimming with all his friends and somehow cut his foot when he was in the lake. His girlfriend wanted to stay and watch the kids' games, but Brian was already walking towards home. After they left, all my anxiety left and I started the kids games. My mom and I are in charge of all the kids' games. We break them up into different age groups. Then there are prizes for all the kids when it is done. We made it through as many as we could until a big gust of wind came through. The sky turned dark and everyone was scrambling to get their belongings and pack up before the storm came. I'm home now watching the storm from inside. I always love a good storm. My hand is cramping up from writing. I will write more another time.

Erin

AUGUST, 2003 9:30 P.M.

Something totally unexpected happened this evening while walking Chance. I was walking him along the highway near my house in Wisconsin. We were walking near the cornfields when a blue truck came by and honked. It was going by so fast I didn't get time to see who it was. When I got further down the street, I could see the truck in my grandparents' driveway. When I made it to the driveway I noticed a guy with his back to me in the back of the pick up truck. I thought it was one of my uncles so decided to walk up the driveway and find out. Suddenly the man turned around and it was Brian. It was too late to turn around and no one else was around. I looked past him and saw Grandpa in the garage and shouted to him. "Hi Grandpa!" Brian was with Mike also. Mike came walking up and began talking to me. My heart was pounding and I didn't know what to say. So I turned to Brian and said, "What are you guys doing?" He responded by saying they were dropping some furniture off and borrowed a family friend's truck. Mike began talking to me and I continued to talk to him just so I didn't have to stand there not saying anything with Brian five feet in front of me. Brian jumped from the truck and believe it or not walked closer to me and began petting Chance. At this point I thought I was dreaming. I couldn't believe he just walked up and began petting Chance. The funny part was Brian didn't know how bad Chance smelled. Although since I don't have my sense of smell it doesn't bother me at all. I've seen the reactions of people who have smelled their hand after petting him and it wasn't a pretty sight. So I let him pet Chance and figured he find out later when he put his hand near his face. After about five minutes I made my exit to leave and they all said goodbye. Walking down towards the beach I was in shock at what just took place. I had no time to think. I just wanted to get the heck away from there. Then I began to think about it some more and feel maybe it was meant to be that I ran into Brian. In the past whenever I saw Brian's car or him I would turn around, but since they were driving a truck I had never seen before and beeped at me, it grabbed my attention. I think it was God's way of making me take a step forward in life by crossing paths with Brian.

Erin

SEPTEMBER, 2003 9:30 P.M.

School has started and I am a senior in high school this year. My favorite class will be creative writing. My least favorite will be Algebra 2. I am retaking it again. Hopefully I will pass this year. I got A's in Geometry. Algebra just isn't for me. I do well in all my other classes. I ended last year with a B in Chemistry, which is a tough course. I'm taking Psychology this year, which should be a fun class. It will prepare me for college when I am taking similar classes for my social work degree. The nice thing about going into social work is the field is so big. You can work in schools, hospitals, non-profit organizations, nursing homes, or police departments, just about anywhere. I've spent the past three years of high school dealing with my past. I want to spend this last year and make it the best. A school year I can look back on and remember forever.

Erin

SEPTEMBER, 2003 11:00 P.M.

Things have not been going well at all. I made it through the summer, but just before school started I began having panic attacks. They are ten times worse then the flashbacks. My heart begins to beat fast, my hands become sweaty, my breathing feels like it is being cut off, and my body shakes. The first time it happened I went to the bathroom and threw up. Well ever since then every time I have a panic attack I run to the bathroom and throw up. It is a horrible experience. I recently told Mrs. Ardell and Dr. Stern. They are both trying to think of relaxation and breath exercises for me, but I am sick of living like this. It just isn't fair. I feel like I have no control over my life, never knowing when a panic attack or flashback will occur. I've been getting out more and taking long walks with Chance. My favorite time to take walks is when the sun is setting or the sky is full of stars. Everything around me is peaceful and quiet. I want to conquer these panic attacks and flashbacks and move on with my life. I wrote Brian recently and asked him to talk over the phone. He responded by saying he is getting settled down in college and he will contact me when he is ready. It will be the first time in five years I will speak to Brian. I told Dr.

Stern about it and she feels it might help me. So now I just wait to hear back from him.

Erin

SEPTEMBER, 2003 11:30 P.M.

I experienced a panic attack tonight and writing eases my tension. It is so hard to breath. My heart beats so fast and my whole body shakes when I sit down. Before it happened I was at dinner with my parents. Right before we were about to leave, a panic attack started. I tried taking deep breaths to control it, but it wasn't working. My parents didn't notice anything until we got out in the parking lot as we were leaving and I turned to my mom and told her I feel like I am going to puke. She could see the look in my face and pulled me over into the grass where I began throwing up. Mom thought I was dehydrated and that is why I was throwing up. She doesn't know about the panic attacks I have. They are much worse than the flashbacks. I have absolutely no control over my body. When we got home I couldn't stop shaking and my heart was racing. I stepped outside to get some fresh air, but nothing was working. Eventually mom told me to suck on ice. I got a cup of ice and went back up into the bathroom where I was lying on the floor. I began crying as I put ice in my mouth. I ran a cold washrag under water and placed it over my face. Slowly I started to breathe easier and my breathing slowed down. I eventually climbed into bed where I am now. A panic attack makes me very tired afterwards. It feels like I have had a workout when it is over. I am exhausted and ready for bed. God, please hold me in your arms tonight. I need your comfort.

Erin

OCTOBER, 2003 10:00 P.M.

Suddenly a flash of images runs through my mind. My body feels trapped and paralyzed. Screaming to get out. I'm standing in the corner of a room watching a girl about the age of twelve. She looks a lot like me when I was twelve. I then notice tears running down her cheeks. She looks me in the eyes with a look begging for help. I notice the man sitting on her being very sexual. She lies helplessly staring at me as tears continue to fall from her face. "I'm sorry," I tell her. "Please forgive me for not saving you." I sit in silence as I watch myself being abused at twelve years old feeling so helpless. The room so silent only the sounds of his heavy breathing against my ear.

"Erin, snap out of it!" my friend shouts at me. "You're staring off into space and didn't even notice us leaving." Another day stuck in my past.

Erin

OCTOBER, 2003 7:00 P.M.

It all began fifth period yesterday. I sat in class as the teacher lectured and began feeling a panic attack coming. I didn't know how to escape it. I sat silently staring at the floor. My legs start to move up and down rapidly and I can't stop them. A student gets the teacher's attention. "Something is wrong with Erin. She looks like she is going to puke," a student says. The teacher finishes her lesson plans and comes up to talk to me. I am trapped and cannot speak. The teacher pulls a desk out into the hall to speak with me. I don't respond back. She goes looking for Mrs. Ardell. I get up and walk to the bathrooms. I enter, but stop myself. I can't continue to do this to myself. Throwing up is only going to make things worse. I walk back towards the class-room where my teacher is talking to another teacher. "Erin, she is going to walk you down to talk with your counselor." I walk silently down the hallway to the guidance office try-ing to fight off the images in my head. I sit at a seat while the teacher goes looking for my counselor. My counselor comes out and tries talking to me. Once again I can't find my voice. I am trapped inside my head with images running through it. I hear my counselor and struggle to talk to her. She walks me down to the nurse. "Erin, how about you lie down until we can locate Mrs. Ardell," my counselor said. I walked into the small, dark room and curled up in a ball on the bed. The tears streaming down my face and all I could think about doing was ending my life. For the next half hour I lay in the dark planning my own death. I decided sleeping pills was the best way out. I still had a full bottle from this summer when I stopped taking them. My plan was, after everyone went to sleep, to take out my goodbye letter from underneath my mattress. I don't like calling it a suicide letter. I was to leave it on the kitchen counter where my father would discover it in the morning. I then would go up in my room with a full glass of water and one by one swallow the bottle of sleeping pills. Like every other night I would bring Chance upstairs and have him sleep at the end of my bed for one last night. I would ask God to forgive me of my sins and turn off my light. I guessed within a few hours after turning off my light I'd be in peace in Heaven. My heart still beating fast, I try calming myself, but I'm too worked up. Suddenly I feel the hand of someone on my back. "Erin, you're ok." I recognize the voice. "Does your mom know you are in here?" I shake my head no and realize it is Mrs. Ardell. She leaves and says she'll be right back. A couple minutes later Mrs. Ardell returns with my mom. The two of them tell me to take some deep breaths. Mom gets up and gets me a glass of water. Within a few minutes my heart stops pounding and my breathing slows down. Mrs. Ardell begins to talk to mom about how much I am struggling. My mom agrees that something more needs to be done. The two of them decide to go call Dr. Stern. They got Dr. Stern's voice mail and left a message. They felt it best if I go home, but they both felt it would be unsafe if they sent me home by myself. Mrs. Ardell had another meeting to run to, but asked me to stop down at her office during seventh hour. Mom had to get back to her post, but said she'd be back in an hour. By now the light was on and they both closed the door behind them. I tried pulling out my journal, but didn't feel like writing. I then pulled out a book I'm reading, but didn't feel up to reading either. I was physically and emotionally exhausted. Instead I sat wondering what was next step in my life to over come my past. I then began to wonder what a scene I must have made in class, in the hall, and in the guidance office. I start to think about the past five years and how much of it has been spent caught up in the abuse. I then begin to wonder how my family will be affected after I am gone. "Will they be angry with me, hate me, or will they be able to understand I couldn't go on?" I ask myself. I once heard that killing yourself is selfish. I don't want to be known as being selfish. I have been fighting this battle for too many years. I am physically and emotionally drained. The door opens and mom walks in. Mom walked me down to Mrs. Ardell's office and told me to come find her when I'm done. When I reach Mrs. Ardell's office I sit down and she listens to her voice mail. Dr. Stern had called back. Mrs. Ardell makes a call to Dr. Stern. I sit and listen as she jots down notes. About five minutes pass when their conversation ends. Mrs. Ardell begins explaining to me the plan. "It's time you get the care

you need. We feel it best if we get you into the hospital."
Trying to hold back from crying again I hear Mrs. Ardell ask
me what I am thinking about. "I just want to be healthy and
happy. I want my life back," I tell her. I'm so exhausted from
living in this constant battle with my past. With a gentle kind
voice Mrs. Ardell said, "I understand you're frustrated. I
would be too. I think this is the best thing for you right now."
She then begins to write down notes that she wants me to
give to mom. Dr. Stern wants mom to call my Psychiatrist,
Dr. Paul and then call the behavioral health hospital when
we get home. Mrs. Ardell finishes up and wishes me good
luck. Just as I am walking out the door Mrs. Ardell says my
name, "Erin, remember baby steps. Take this one day at a
time." Thinking about what Mrs. Ardell said I make my way
downstairs to find my mom. Mom signs me out and we both
leave school early. When we got home mom called my psychiatrist who made an appointment for tomorrow to see me
and then told mom to call the hospital and set up a time to
get an assessment. That night mom filled Dad in on what
happened. I knew ending my life at this point would be like
giving up. I decided to give the hospital a chance and see
what it might have to offer me. The next day mom and I left
school early for a forty-five minute drive to my psychiatrist's
office. My psychiatrist put me on a new medication to help
with the flashbacks. She then explained she would meet up
with me in the hospital Monday to see how things are going.
On the way out of her office we ran into Dr. Stern. She asked
how I was doing and we cancelled my appointment for next
Monday since I was going to be in the hospital. She wished
me luck and mom and I left. My appointment with the hospital wasn't for another two hours so mom and I went out to
eat. While at dinner we talked a lot about everything that
was going on. After dinner we drove to the hospital. We

entered the hospital and took a seat in the waiting room. After waiting an hour I was finally brought back. After the entire assessment was over mom was brought back. Because of my age I could either go in either the adolescent or adult unit. We all agreed the adult would be better for me. We also decided partial hospitalization was the best route to go. I spend the entire day in the hospital, but go home at night. They had to process everything with the insurance company and said that I would begin Tuesday instead of Monday. When we got home we packed up for the weekend. We were leaving for Wisconsin and then in the morning going to Minnesota to visit Catilin in college. I've had a long day and need to get some sleep. We have a seven-hour drive in the morning.

Erin

OCTOBER, 2003 8:30 P.M.

Tomorrow I start at the hospital. I am really nervous. I hope I don't feel out of place or anything. This weekend while in Minnesota, Allie and me spent the night at Catilin's apartment while mom and dad stayed in a hotel. I met her roommates and another girl who had been in a behavioral hospital before. She filled me in on what it was like, making me feel a little more at ease about tomorrow. Then Caitlin decides we all need to watch "Girl Interrupted." The whole movie is filmed in a mental hospital with a bunch of crazy people. I guess it was my way of preparing myself. I will write about the first day tomorrow.

Erin

OCTOBER, 2003 8:00 P.M.

I pulled up in the parking lot of the hospital and parked my car. I sat in the car debating whether to go inside. It was a beautiful sunny day as I finally stepped out into the sunlight and headed for the hospital doors. I walked in and up to the reception desk and was told to take a seat on the couch and someone would be with me shortly. I focus my attention on the television, which has the "Today Show" on. Suddenly I hear my name being called. I look to see an older man standing there. I walk towards him and he introduces himself to me and shows me towards the electronic locked doors that are operated by the front desk. I am walked into the cafeteria and told to take a seat at the booth. I notice his nametag that read Bill. He begins explaining all the paper work I must fill out. He tells me he'll be back later to check in on me. After he walked away I skim through all the paper work he has just given me. For the next hour I sit filling out questions, surveys, medical history, and had to sign a bunch of documents. Bill soon returns and sits down with me. He begins reading through my information. I begin to feel really uncomfortable when he begins mentioning I was sexually abused. I've never been one to talk to men about my past. I grow tense hoping the questions will soon end. After two hours of paper work and questions Bill gives me my schedule for the week. He then shows me where my first group will begin. I begin the day with stress management group. I listen in as therapists explain ways of managing stress. We were given a worksheet to fill out on preparing for an upcoming stressful situation. I identified Thanksgiving where I'll see Brian. I then had to plan out my safety, security, physical health and well being. It asked how you'd cope with overwhelmed feelings. I feel I will take some deep breaths and step out of the room if necessary. At noon it was time for lunch. The therapist asked someone to buddy up with me and show me around the cafeteria. We all were handed a ticket and walked down a few halls. I stood in line holding my tray and once I got to the counter asked for chicken and a bowl of soup. For hospital food it wasn't bad. I sat in a booth as other woman asked me why I was in the hospital. I told them a little about my past and they were supportive. I looked around the cafeteria at the different people around me. At one table sat a group of really skinny teenagers whom I assumed were dealing with eating disorders. Behind them was a group of teenage boys and girls who had piercing and dyed hair. I later learned they were the co-dependency group. I stare at the expressions on faces and can see the pain in their eyes. So many are hurting like me. Outside people sit at tables and eat their lunch while being monitored.

After lunch I learned about assertiveness. Learning how to make "I feel" and "I want" statements. We then talked about aggressive, passive, and passive-aggressive behavior. I see myself being very passive, but that is where my problem is. I'm avoiding the conflict of my past. Looking for the easy way out. I'd rather focus my energy on someone else then take a good hard look in the mirror at myself. The last group of the day was expressive therapy and it was my favorite. I took a seat at the table along with everyone else. The room was filled with all kinds of art supplies and games. There was a window that let the sun shine in from the outside. The expressive therapist was a skinny Korean woman who was very supportive. She handed out thick white pieces of paper to everyone. She placed watercolor paint on the desks and asked us to paint anything we wanted and told us we'd talk about our paintings at the end of the hour. I sat holding the paintbrush starring outside at the sky. Big, fluffy, white clouds came and went reminding me of cotton candy as a kid. I finally decided to paint butterflies and write positive, uplifting words to motivate myself. The butterflies represent when I was younger when the abuse was going on. I watched a movie called "Radio Flyer" and in my head created my own fantasy of being able to create my own Radio Flyer and escape the abuse I was being faced with. Remembering "Radio Flyer" was like being able to pretend to escape my abuse. I even had my own place I imagined in my head where I would take my Radio Flyer to make my final escape. A very quiet and peaceful place where no one would find me. Nothing but trees, green grass, and the sunset. After finishing the paintings we took turns talking about them just before it was time to leave. The first day was finally over. I walked out into the parking lot to my car. I had survived my first day in the hospital and just wanted to go home and sleep. I will do the same thing tomorrow. Get up and start a new day.

Erin

OCTOBER, 2003 3:00 P.M.

It is day two at the hospital. I went to goals and processing group in the morning. I don't want to be here anymore. I don't belong. I am surrounded by a bunch of people who are miserable. One lady constantly rocks back and forth. Another lady cries for no apparent reason. There is even one woman who talks about killing herself every two minutes. I just don't feel this is right for me, but Mrs. Ardell warned me it would be hard at first. I promised her that I would not give up so instead I am just going to focus on myself. I just want to find the happiness that has been gone for so many years. I talked to my case manager today and began crying. I told her how I just want to live a normal life and not live in my past. She gave me a worksheet where I fill in my own relaxation place that I create. She wants me to use it in stressful situations when I am feeling overwhelmed. After coming home from the hospital, all I want to do is go to bed.

Erin

OCTOBER, 2003 9:00 P.M.

I started my day like every other day with goals and processing group. My process issue was learning to forgive. I'm sick of living with so much anger and hate. I just can't imagine myself ever finding the courage to forgive Brian. He took so much from me. I then went to victim/survivor group. I wrote down victim/survivor statements. My survivor statement was, "I am a survivor and I can accomplish anything." Soon it was lunch and I had pasta with a roll. At lunch I sat with the same women I sit with every day, but a man who was twenty joined us after learning that he had to find healthy new friendships. I suggested trying Willow Creek Church. I told him what a great church it was. After lunch I went to expressive therapy. We played charades. The expressive therapist began by acting them out. We eventually started doing our own. I'd motion with my hands I was doing a movie. I then began acting out the movie "Girl Interrupted." When the group finally figured it out the therapist began laughing. I went on to do "Twenty-Eight Days," "One Flew Over the Cuckoo's Nest," and "What About Bob." Everyone got a good laugh out of it. I ended my day at the hospital talking about boundaries, learning to set up boundaries. Boundaries help to create safety. I'm learning to set up boundaries for myself. I need to get some rest now. I have the Chicago marathon this Sunday.

Erin

OCTOBER, 2003 11:45 P.M.

It's Friday night and I've completed one week at the hospital. We worked on weekend planning and skills group today. Learning different skills to work with in our daily lives. I also had expressive therapy in the gym. The expressive therapist had us lie on mats and listen to a deep relaxation tape. It put all my worries aside. I'm now trying to prepare myself for the Chicago marathon this Sunday. Twenty-six miles in all. By Sunday night I will have accomplished more then I could ever imagine.

Erin

OCTOBER, 2003 7:30 P.M.

It has been an amazing day. Although my muscles and body ache as I write this, I've never felt more proud in my life. Standing on the streets of Chicago with forty thousand other people waiting for the race to start. The city is so big and it was a perfect day for a marathon. The weather was great. The sky was blue and the sun was shining bright. When the race started I looked around at the media, people holding signs, and even young children cheering everyone on. Having the encouragement from the sidewalks kept me moving. At mile marker two a boy around nine years old said, "You're almost there." I found it very funny and so did the people around me. I met up with two women named Pat and Jean at the beginning of the race and stuck with them the entire twenty-six miles. I had split up from our marathon team, so when I met up with Jean and Pat, it was nice to talk to someone throughout the race. They kept me from quitting. At times we would be so exhausted that we would sing. One of the songs we would sing was "Row, Row, Row Your Boat." We would eventually run out of air from singing and all start giggling. I felt so proud of myself after every mile completed. Printed on some buildings was a sign that said, "Some people won't even drive 26 miles today." There were signs like this everywhere. It was so amazing to see all the different people that came out to cheer the runners and walkers on. From the little kids to the old senior citizens. There were even homeless people standing and watching. I passed areas where people made there own drums and other music out of pots and pans. We would pass the different water and Gatorade stations as people cheered us on. Our shoes would stick to the pavement from the spilled Gatorade. The tall sky scrapers were like huge walls and each one I passed was like another wall I knocked down in my life. Each mile was like a different stage of my life. It was like walking down the journey of my past. After all, what brought me to volunteer at the Advocacy Center to begin with was my past. What kept me going and made me cross the finish line was what I was doing it all for. I had raised over seven hundred dollars for children who had been abused. It was for these children and the child I once was that I finished the race today. My inner child didn't give up on me. The last mile was the hardest. I never thought I'd see the finish line. Just when I was ready to give up, I turned the corner and could see the finish line in the distance. When I crossed it, a medal was placed around my neck and my picture was taken. Finishing the Chicago marathon has given me strength and made me a stronger person. The only difference between the first person that crossed hours earlier and when I crossed was they were walking home two-hundred-and-fifty-thousand-dollars richer. In my eyes money doesn't buy happiness. So I was proud of the fact I finished. Now I am facing the aftermath of barely being able to walk, and my feet are covered in blisters. No matter what, I don't regret a thing. I would do it again tomorrow! Ok, maybe not tomorrow, but I would do it again. When I got home from this evening, mom was crying and had flowers and gifts for me. She hugged me and told me how proud she was of me. I am very tired and am going to bed early. Night!

Erin

OCTOBER, 2003 8:00 P.M.

It is Tuesday night. It was my last day at the hospital today. I am supposed to finish the week off, but I feel I got what I needed out of the hospital. I need to get back to school. Although I was extremely sore Monday after the marathon, I still went to the hospital. The patients and staff were all congratulating me. Yesterday I ended the day with expressive therapy and drew a picture of a very bright sunset. It brought peace to me and made me feel good inside. I talked to my psychiatrist yesterday and told her I felt that I got what I needed out of the hospital. The idea was for me to come twice a week, but I told her I want to be done completely.

Usually you have to step down in the program, but my psychiatrist agreed with me and said, "If that is what I want to do then she'll sign the paper work." Since today was my last day I did a lot of talking in process group. I also helped a woman in the group and the therapist later told me I did an awesome job in group therapy. By now I know everyone really well. While in the gym we started doing different body motions pretending to be someone. Very similar to the movie "Girl Interrupted." I was trying to hold back from laughing because I found it very funny. The funniest part was to see how serious and intense the expressive therapist was. You could tell she puts a lot of effort into her job. I had to leave and go to the bathroom at one point I was laughing so hard. I thought this only happened in movies, not in real life. I think I would go insane if I was upstairs in lock down. I'd have no freedom then. When the day was done everyone wished me good luck and I wished everyone good luck in their future. I told them I enjoyed the time over the week and a half I spent with them. My case manager wished me good luck in the future. She gave me some paper work to sign and gave me some information to keep. I looked over what she gave me before leaving. I read that the main focus of my treatment was stabilizing the Post Traumatic Stress Disorder. Today for one last time I left the hospital and walked out into the parking lot and for the first time proud of my progress.

Erin

OCTOBER, 2003 10:15 P.M.

I returned to school today and everyone was asking me where I was this past week. I lied to many people and told them I was on vacation. How do you tell someone you were in a lock-down mental hospital? They would look at me as if I were crazy. Well, they already think I'm crazy so it wouldn't matter. Mental health has a bad enough stigma to begin with. I ran into Mrs. Ardell before school even started and she was shocked to see me. She wasn't expecting to see me until the following week. I also talked to Dr. Stern for the first time since I was placed in the hospital. I filled her in on how everything went. I got a load of homework I need to make up. I also have tests to make up to. I hate being behind. I'll write more when I get time.

Erin

OCTOBER, 2003 9:00 P.M.

Today at school the school social worker Mrs. Haas told me about The Clothesline Project coming to our school today. It is a project where survivors of sexual violence express themselves on T-shirts. I went down during my lunch with another girl and read the shirts. Some were so graphic with writings. It is a bunch of shirts with a lot of pain expressed on them all hanging on a clothesline. I later went up to the guidance office the last period of the day and Mrs. Haas set me up with a T-shirt and puffy paint. At first I sat starring at the T-shirt wondering how I could put into words how I felt about Brian and my abuse. I finally let my hand do the work and began putting down my pain and anger. "I am a survivor not your victim" was the best statement on mine. There were other girls in the room making shirts as well. After finishing the shirt I felt a sense of relief, being able to express myself like that in a healthy way. I walked away feeling good about myself.

OCTOBER, 2003 9:30 P.M.

I can't believe I am writing this. I never thought I would write this. I just got off the phone with Brian and I'm not kidding. This is how it all happened. A few days ago I received an e-mail from Brian telling me he is ready to talk on the phone. A day later we set up a time and day, which happened to be tonight. I was terrified to make the call. I dialed and hung up four or five times before hearing the phone ring. It rang five or six times before he picked up. I heard him say hello and could tell he was nervous. The conversation lasted about a half hour and it was just small talk. I just let him know what an impact his actions have had on my life and he let me know that he is a changed man. He tried telling me about his life over the years and how his actions have always hung over him. I kept the conversation simple and didn't get into much because it was the first time in five years we were speaking. I did ask him if he ever told his girlfriend and he told me that she heard about it at school and asked him about it and he told her it was true. I doubt Brian told her how abusive he really was. In fact I am sure he denied it all. He tried telling me he has changed his life around and is involved with volunteer work and even signed up to be a volunteer as a Big Brother for a child. Hearing that made my stomach turn into knots. All I could think was another innocent child being abused.

Towards the end of our conversation he mentioned how he couldn't believe how calm I was. He said he was expecting me to be hysterical with him. I told him I have a lot of anger and hate towards him, but getting angry on the phone would resolve nothing. I finished by saying, "I am trying to let go of some of this anger and hate. Holding on to it is only hurting me more." I told him I've been waiting a long time for a meaningful apology and want him to put some thought into it before coming out and apologizing. Before Brian hung up he told me if and when I want to talk again just e-mail him and we would set up a time to talk. I had God with me the entire night. I don't know how I made it through the half an hour without freaking out. Being able to let Brian know how much pain he has caused me was empowering. I now pray he will come to me and apologize. I am proud that I have taken this huge step and finally talked with him on the phone. I will sleep well tonight. It just doesn't seem real that I talked to him. I'll be playing that conversation over in my head all night.

Erin

NOVEMBER, 2003 9:30 P.M.

For years now I've wondered if I'd ever hear Brian apologize. Having to see him at holidays throughout the years has always torn me up inside and memories have haunted me all these years. I never expected myself to confront Brian back in April. I never imagined being placed in a hospital. The thought of ever talking to Brian on the phone never even crossed my mind. My number one prayer for years now is to move on with my life and forgive Brian. In a way it seemed impossible without Brian apologizing and asking for forgiveness. I've been telling Brian since April that when he is truly sorry and wants forgiveness to let me know. Today was a day I've waited five long years for. I received a letter from Brian that made me break down and cry. A letter I thought I'd never receive. All my emotions are pouring out of me right now.

Erin,

For the last four or five years I had wondered if you really had accepted my first apology at Bill's house. I was pretty certain that you hadn't due to all the looks that have been exchanged between you and me at family parties. Over the last five years there has just been a complete lack of comfort and true enjoyment at family gatherings. That is one strong reason that I wished you had forgiven me. Every time before a family event I always hoped that you weren't going to be there because I just didn't want to feel terrible and uncomfortable. It wasn't that I minded you, what I hated was the stale air between us. That is something I could probably stand to live with the rest of my life though. What I hate living with is the fact that I destroyed your life.

I would assume that if you never forgive me for my actions that over time you will build this hate and this rage would in turn spark a need or want for revenge. I do not know if this would happen, but I do know that if it did it would consume your life and mine. All I want is for all of us to go on living a much happier life as well as a more satisfying one. I know that when you get a thought of me it probably consumes your thoughts and feelings for a long extent because when I used to hear your name or if I was talking to someone about my cousins, my thoughts and emotions would rip into me for more than a day because I really felt that I had fucked up your life as well as mine. I pray that someday this feeling goes away. I hope one day that I feel satisfied enough that I haven't destroyed the rest of your life. I believe that will only come when you have accepted my apology.

A couple years ago I apologized and I will do it again. Erin I am sorry for what I did to you. My actions weren't thought out, I was confused and disoriented, and I acted on the behalf of just plain stupidity. I wish that I had never hurt you the way I did. I wish I could go back into my past and stop myself and teach myself what was wrong with my actions, but I had to learn the hard way and unfortunately you were the one I abused. I apologize for the past and I hope that you can forgive me, but if you can't, I can understand. I am sorry.

Brian

I'm speechless! I wasn't expecting to ever hear this. Receiving this letter has opened a whole new door in my life a door that has been locked for a long time. I now feel I can look to the future and not live in the past. I realize how fortunate I am to be able to have communication with my abuser. There are so many more victims of abuse who don't have this opportunity that I have to confront their abuser and then get a letter asking for forgiveness. It all seems too unreal. For once I can see the light at the end of the tunnel. I see myself reaching the end of this road proud of myself that I never gave up. I look out the window and see a shooting star across the sky. A star I prayed on for many years. Thank you, God! Thank You!

Erin

NOVEMBER, 2003 8:15 P.M.

Brian,

I've struggled over the past weeks to write this letter to you. I never imagined the day I'd be faced with writing this letter. If you were to ask me a couple months ago if I would be willing to forgive you in my lifetime I'd say no. The pain you have caused me has been unbearable at times. The memories I must live with the rest of my life that can't be erased. It has taken a lot of thought and soul searching to finally put it on paper. I'll begin by saying no matter how many times I tell you the pain you caused me, you'll never be able to understand the depth of your actions in my life. No apology can erase the effects of your actions, nor can it bring back the precious years you took from me. Although the abuse may have ended when I was thirteen, the memories will last a lifetime.

The emotional roller coaster I've been on the past five years has been nothing but a world of hell. Hell that has caused me to harm myself through self-injury. I'd rather feel the physical pain then the emotional scars you've left on my life that bring me down a terrible road of trauma. No matter, the anger you have caused me will never leave. I will always be angry for what you did to me. Your actions have played such a role in my life that there have been times where my only hope is to end it all by taking my own life. I soon realized that ending my life through suicide would only let you win again. You already robbed me of my childhood; I couldn't die knowing you were the one that caused me to end it all. You may have taken my innocence, ability to trust, an incredible family relationship, you even robbed me of my childhood, but, Brian, you have not destroyed my life. If you have destroyed anyone's life, it is your own. For you must live with yourself the rest of your life knowing what you've done.

I've spent countless hours in therapy trying to unravel the mess you put me through. I am at a point where I will continue to look back and put the pieces together of my childhood, but in the end I will still be left with questions I may never get answers to. I'm going on with my life and no longer living as your victim, but instead as a true survivor. I will hold on to the precious years when I knew no evil and my childhood was anything a child would want. In my heart I believe everyone is born a good person. I once knew the good person you were. You made some terrible mistakes in your past and I hope that hearing the pain you placed on me has opened your eyes. As for the person you tell me you are today, I'm hearing a man who feels terrible for his actions and wants to move on with his life and wants to be forgiven for his actions. Brian, as much as I have hated you over the years and wanted you to suffer the way I have, it was all out of anger and I had every right to be angry. Brian, only you know in your heart if you are honestly sorry and a changed man. I can't trust your word that you have changed nor will I ever trust anything you say. Brian, only you know the true you. I will worry when you become a father someday. I can only hope you'll be a good father and bring no harm to another child. So I hope if you ever feel the urge to hurt someone again you'll do the right thing and get yourself help, the best thing you could ever do for yourself. When I first contacted you back in April, I told you I pray for the children you might father someday. I now pray for those children and for your soul. To give you the strength to move on with your life the way God is giving me the strength to move on with mine. I will leave it in God's hands for he knows the real you that I don't.

I will live with the memories the rest of my life, I will take the pain you caused me to my grave someday, and as for the hate, I will not. For the first time I can tell you I forgive you and mean it. I only want you to accept it if you are truly a changed man and will never harm another innocent person again. People make mistakes, and I feel and hope that your past was just a mistake that you are learning from. I can forgive you, but God makes the final judgment. I'll end it by saying now that I am willing to forgive you; I suggest you now ask God for forgiveness. I will be praying for you. You're forgiven!

Erin

THANKSGIVING, 2003 11:40 P.M.

I sat down for the first time in years at a table filled with turkey, stuffing, mashed potatoes, cranberries, corn, and a table filled with people. One of those people was my cousin Brian. Someone I have avoided for years and feared. I now can look across the table at him and not cringe. In the past my stomach turned to knots. This year was different. I felt peace when I looked at Brian and he said, "Hello, Happy Thanksgiving." I felt that I had conquered my greatest challenge. I confronted my biggest fear and in the end found peace. I gained back the control and power Brian had taken from me when I was 11 years old.

We sat down as a family and bowed our heads to give thanks. As I bowed my head I could feel God's presence surrounding me, giving me a pat on the back. I thank Him for never giving up on me when I doubted him. For the first time since I was a child I am thankful. Thankful to be alive. Thankful God never gave up on me. Thankful for the strength and courage I've been given. I never imagined it could be possible that I could forgive Brian and speak to him again. I've learned in life anything is possible. Tonight as I turn out my light I give thanks to everyone that has helped me down this road to healing and I pray for the children and adults that will be faced with the same journey I've faced growing up. Good night!

Erin

A Mother's Words

"Of all the rights of women,
the greatest is to be a mother."

—Lin Yutang

January, 2004 7:30 a.m.

An entry from my mom

Watching your child carrying the weight of being sexually abused is a pain that is unbearable. It is a helpless feeling knowing you cannot soothe their pain or take this weight from them. You cannot ease the pain with an aspirin or treat the wound with a salve. The injury to your child is so deep and hard to reach that it deems you helpless in doing the job as a "mother". Mother, the one who kisses your wounds and nurses you back to health. Had it not been for my Christian faith I don't think I could have managed or faced this crisis.

I too was sexually abused in my youth and know all too well the ongoing effects it has on your life. Like a nail driven into a piece of wood. The nail can be removed but the hole it creates will always remain.

When I first learned about the crime committed against my daughters, it was as if someone punched me in the gut.

A wave of nausea fell upon me and I wanted to throw up the truth of it. In that moment I felt like my whole being was short-circuiting. My life was shaken and thrown off course. My mind had too many places to go all at once. It was like switching a television channel to a high drama war scene and being snatched off the comfort of my sofa with no armor or weapons. Unarmed and confused I wondered, "How did I get here. What do I do now?" My mind a stage with all the players wanting to act at once, shock, anger sadness, pain, guilt, helplessness, loathing and rage.

I found my own childhood abuse being triggered. I didn't need a textbook explanation on how this was affecting my girls. I also knew that I needed to do everything in my power to help restore them. Starting with the message that "they mattered". No one, and I mean NO ONE, violates you and gets away with it. Regardless of how sensitive the crime is. A crime has been committed and the perpetrator would be held accountable. God entrusted Dan and me with three wonderful girls to raise, protect and love. I take the job very seriously. As a mother I feel that I have the greatest job in the world. To be able to stay home and help in the guidance and love of another human being, now that's an honor! However, when hearing of the crime committed against my girls at the hands of a trusted family member, I felt like I had failed them and failed God. I was also a little miffed at God for not protecting them. I had prayed thousands of times for my girls to be protected. I asked God to send the strongest and mightiest guardian angels to watch over them. Why had they been harmed? No sooner was the question asked when I felt His comforting love. God had never failed me and He wasn't about to leave me at this moment. The entire essence of the Bible is stories of incredible hardships and tragedy and how through God these things change into miraculous stories of power, courage, love and hope. These stories all had one thing in common. **Faith.**

Trust in the Lord with all your heart and lean not to your own understanding. In all your ways acknowledge Him and He shall direct your paths.

Proverbs 3:5–6.

All things work together for good to them that love God and are called according to His purpose.

Romans 8:28

My relationship with God and all the years I had read the Bible allowed me to conclude one thing. I needed to have faith, and trust Him. However, I must say, the anger I felt towards Brian did not lift. I definitely related to Christ's anger in the temple. I was in for a few years of throwing tables in my soul. I knew that it would take time. Healing takes time and patience. I prayed for God to be with Erin and that she would feel His presence.

Especially when Erin shut me out, not wanting to talk with me about her pain. I felt a deep sense of helplessness and failure. I couldn't understand why she wouldn't let me help her through it. Especially since I understood her pain all too well. It wasn't until she explained to me that she needed me to hold the good things in her life, the happy moments. She didn't want to taint our relationship with all her pain. I finally understood, and had to let go, letting her get the help she needed elsewhere, in a safe place. Years ago while I was consumed in my own personal pain I realized that throughout my life during the moments that I was the saddest were the times I didn't call upon God for help. Feeling stuck, wallowing in a pity-party. Sometimes it took several days until I would finally call upon God for guidance. And His comfort and answers were always there. I finally asked God if He would do something for me. I asked if, in those moments of pain and despair, if He would send me a sign to put me in remembrance that He was there with me. I asked Him, "Lord, send me a sign in nature, something in your creation that would draw my attention away from my crisis and back to you." Well, ask and you shall receive. I could write a short novel on how God delivered that request.

Over the years my life has been filled with "gifts of nature" in hard times. Everything from flocks of geese landing at my feet, encircling me in a parking lot, to a monarch butterfly landing on my nose amidst my tear-stained cheeks. One afternoon as I sat on the edge of our deck worrying about one thing or another, a skunk interrupted my dilemma by crawling right out from under the deck between my legs. These moments never cease to amaze me, and they always put a smile back on my face and a light in my heart.

The nature message that has had the biggest impact on my life was one morning a few years after the abuse to my daughters. I was sitting in our yard at our lake house. My anger towards Brian and the reactions of my husband's family were overwhelming me. It was consuming my life, my happiness. At that moment, in this small side yard appeared three squirrels chasing each other around the tree. Out from the pine trees hopped a small baby rabbit. Five yellow finches landed on the tree along with a cardinal and her mate. A chipmunk jumped out from the flowerbed. A morning dove cooed from the pines above and a monarch butterfly fluttered in and joined the show. My spirit lifted and I praised God for His never ending care and love for me.

I thanked Him for being there and showing me all the beauty around me. As I watched the wonders of nature around me, a bee flew towards me and wouldn't leave. He buzzed around my head. I ducked and swayed, flinching at his approach. I waved my arms in the air to combat his attack. Being allergic I feared that I would get stung so I continued to dodge and duck as he swooped down at me This bee almost seemed to be attacking me. It was weird. As I combated the annoyance of the bee, I mumbled to God, "So what's this supposed to mean?" And if you have never had God speak to your heart, it is a distinct message you can't deny and it is not of your own creation. The message was, *"All it takes is one small annoying, painful thing in your life to get your eyes and attention off all the wonderful things I have given you."*

The message was loud and clear. If I keep concentrating all my energy on the thing that pains me, I will miss all the wonderful things in my life. I knew at that moment I had to let go of the anger that consumed me.

Since that day I have tried to keep my eyes open to the beautiful things in my life and one of the most beautiful is my daughter Erin. I see a wonderful young lady that has endured things that most of us can't even imagine. Someone who never gives up and pushes herself as high as she can go. She has a heart of gold. I am in awe at the gift she is to others. I love listening to her experiences as she volunteered at the home for the elderly, working with the Alzheimer's patients. She has so much tenderness and care and patience. I see this also in her volunteer work with children. Erin loves children. She helps mothers in need without wanting pay. She volunteers at the Children's Advocacy center and has even completed the Chicago marathon for this cause. She has gone door-to-door collecting money for a family whose home was burned down in a fire. She stands up for what she believes in. My favorite part of Erin is her faith, her morals and values, and belief in God. She is truly a rare gem. She is truly blessed.

I am so proud of my daughter and all that she has endured and has accomplished, especially writing this book. I know it took many hours of reliving the pain, but I also know Erin wouldn't hesitate to do that if it will help one person through their pain. I love you, Erin.

Mom

Today

"You gain strength, courage, and confidence by each experience in which you really stop to look fear in the face. You are able to say to yourself, 'I have lived through this horror. I can take the next thing that comes along.'"

—Eleanor Roosevelt

TODAY 10:00 P.M.

I woke to the sun hitting my face. I stretched and got up
to the start of the day. I live life with the saying my father
tells me every morning. "Today is the first day of the rest of
your life." After a bowl of "Life" cereal and watching Oprah,
I open the morning paper to read. On the very first page I
read the black bold headline, "Woman sexually assaulted in
broad daylight." Reading through the article I discover the
assault happened just down the street from where I live and
they still have not caught the guy. Turning the next page I
read another headline, "Teacher charged with sexual abuse of
fourth grade student." It saddens me because every day I read
another article in the paper about someone being abused.
The worst part is a majority of the time it is someone the
person trusted. Whether it be a teacher, coach, neighbor,
priest, or in my case, a family member. After having someone
take your trust like that, it is difficult to ever gain it back. I
close the paper and wonder what tomorrow's headlines will

241

be. I grab the leash and head out the door to take Chance on a morning walk. I walk down the path and take in the beauty around me, looking up at the clear blue sky and taking in the crystal clean air. I hear the sounds of birds singing off in the distance. Every now and then I stop to let Chance smell the grass.

As we continued down the path memories of my childhood filled my head. For so many years it was the same path I walked to the elementary school. I remember when Allie, Emily, and I would slide on the ice during winter mornings. I'll never forget the mornings we would be so cold we'd lie on the path because the sun warmed us up. We used to push our baby dolls in our strollers down the path and to the park. Some days we'd ride bikes to school and lock them up at the bike rack. I pass the pond behind my house reminding me of the days when I'd ice skate, go sledding down the hill onto the ice, fish, and take our canoe out. The same pond Chance loves to swim in. Remembering all these childhood memories brings a smile to my face. Knowing I can still hold onto the precious years that meant so much to me, I suddenly come across another place on the path that brings me back to my childhood. Except now I am passing a painful time in my childhood. It is passing my aunt and uncle's house the place where I was abused. I'm not triggered the way I used to be and I don't have a difficult time passing the house. I can still hear my innocent plea for Brian not to hurt me. I continue moving forward down the path, which for a long time was never possible. Times before, going past my aunt and uncles house was a painful reminder. It was like hitting a brick wall. I am no longer turning around and running from my past, too afraid to feel the pain it caused me. Instead I move forward with strength and determination. I come upon a bench and sit down. It is a quiet morning. I only hear the sounds of nature and a plane flying over me. I sit petting the top of Chance's head as he wags his tail. For once I am looking into my soul and seeing all my accomplishments. I've always looked for others to take away my pain when the truth is I needed to look into my soul. Without the support of others I would not be where I am today. For so many years I was running from my past and problems. I finally stopped running and looked at myself in the mirror and realized how miserable I was. I learned it has to come from within to move on with my life. I've lived with so much fear and guilt. I've come to realize I do not need fear to run my life and I have nothing to be guilty about. I've done no wrong. I've always wanted to blame myself about the abuse, but I was just an innocent kid who was being controlled and threatened with fear. My biggest problem all these years has been living as Brian's victim. Victims are weak and I knew I wasn't weak. For I've been a fighter with a lot of strength. Today I consider myself a conqueror. I will be a survivor the rest of my life. For many years I've been trying to get to the end of this journey, in my life. When I finally got to the end of the journey I realized this journey is not over, but instead just the beginning of a lifetime filled with success and determination to go out in the world and tell others my story. A story of how I turned hate into forgiveness. I never thought I'd come to terms with forgiving Brian. Forgiving has been a powerful experience. Finding it in my heart to forgive someone that has caused me the greatest pain in my life. It wasn't easy, but by forgiving Brian it has made me a stronger and bigger person inside.

I know I will never get all the answers to the past. I know I will still face hard times ahead. The memories will always be there and there will be times I will need to step back and take a deep breath. I am prepared for any setbacks in life and know that I can overcome anything. I am not going to let anyone or anything stop me from accomplishing my goals. I've already accomplished things some people won't accomplish in there lifetime. No matter what I do with my life, I will always be proud.

I look to the future now and wonder what lies ahead. I plan to go to college and get my master's in social work, so I can help a child that I once was. I look forward to when I am a mom and can look into my baby's innocent eyes and shower him or her with love. Being a mom will be the greatest job ever.

Tonight Chance and I went for a walk and I could not believe how many stars were in the sky. It was a clear night and the stars were bright, reminding me of summer nights in Wisconsin lying under the stars near a crackling campfire and listening to the crickets in the woods. For once I feel the happiness and peace I never thought I'd see again.

My innocence can't be replaced, and the parts of my childhood can't be relived. I hold on to my innocence and childhood that were memorable and knew no harm, and I am slowly learning to trust again. I love sitting at home on rainy days and watching old home videos of my family and me when we were young. Bringing back the childhood I love to remember. The childhood when I knew no harm.

One thing I haven't lost is my spirit and the courage to heal. Looking into my soul, I used to always see a dark place and I always felt so alone. I never thought I'd see this day. When I look into my soul tonight it is no longer a dark lonely place. It is now a place where I find myself smiling and happy. I finally found the light at the end of the tunnel. I am proud of the person I have become. I've learned that giving up is not an option. I couldn't have seen to the future without the supportive people in my life that never gave up on me. The loving support from both my parents who have helped me along the way. My mom who has had her own trauma as a child and has used her past to help me overcome mine. My father who is one of the hardest working men I know. Going through this life changing experience has brought my Dad and I closer. It has strengthened our relationship. Mrs. Ardell who has given me hope, support, and strength. She has been more then just a school psychologist to me, she has been a friend. Someone I will stay in touch with forever. My therapist who helped me find my inner strength and courage to move on with my life and make healthy choices.

I focus on the future of becoming an advocate for abused children and getting tougher laws on sex offenders. For once I am listening to my inner child and going to do my best to protect other children from having my experience happen to them. I hope to take my story with me to schools and speak out to parents, teachers, and children. If I were given the option to relive my life, I wouldn't take it. I finally understand why I experienced the abuse I endured as a child. God had a plan for me all along. Even though I doubted him in times of my life, He stuck by my side. God knew I would become a stronger person and use my experience to help others. He was right and giving back to others makes me feel proud. There are people in my life that I would never have met had I not been through the experience I faced as a child. I would have never done the Chicago marathon nor would I be a volunteer for the Children's Advocacy Center. I also wouldn't have the passion to help others and spread my word of courage, giving others the faith and wisdom to move on with their life. Sharing my diary has let me open the doors to my soul and share with you my journey to healing and forgiveness. All it took was one night for my entire life to be changed. The permanent scar Brian has left on my life will never go away and I feel by spreading my word about sexual abuse and incest I might just save someone else from experiencing my same pain. My goal in life is to give back and help others, which I've already started. Much of my growing up years have been spent dealing with my childhood. I'm now reaching out and inspiring others. I want to be there for other survivors of abuse. I want them to know that things do get better in time. I know what it feels like when you want to shut the world off and not see tomorrow, but I've learned giving up only makes you weaker. It is ok to ask for help. The biggest mistake I've learned in life is living as a victim. Being a victim gets you nowhere in life. It only makes you weaker.

When someone takes your trust like Brian did to me, it is very difficult to ever give someone your full trust again. I will always have trouble trusting others that come into my life because of my experience as a child, but I won't let it destroy me. After being abused you learn a whole new way of trusting people. It takes much longer and is a lot harder. With April being National Child Abuse Prevention Month it is a month to reach out and prevent child abuse. I plan to spend one day in April every year as a day in silence to reflect on my childhood and honor the lives of millions of other survivors. No matter what, in my eyes Brian will always be a perpetrator and I will have questions for the rest of my life that I may never get answers to. Some may wonder how I was able to forgive Brian who took so much from me. By forgiving Brian it makes me the bigger person. Brian is the only one that knows if he can accept my forgiveness or not, for he is the one who truly knows if he is a changed man. I can't erase what he did, but I can move on. Brian is the one who must live with the guilt and shame for his actions. I leave it in God's hands to guide Brian in the right direction and protect any child that comes into his life. Yes, it will always bother me when he becomes a Dad someday. I can only pray for the best.

If I were to give advice to anyone who has been in my place it would be not to give up. Instead look into your soul where you will find the strength to survive. It comes from within. Don't be a victim of abuse, but instead be a survivor. I finally stopped running from my past and instead turned around and worked through it. No, it wasn't easy, but I did it and because of that I am going to go far in life and be successful. You can't run from your past. It will always catch up to you. It's better to face it head on then to have it come up from behind. It takes some soul searching, but everyone has the strength within them to move on. My name is Erin Merryn and I am a survivor. Tomorrow is a new day and I look to the bright future that lies ahead.

I hope parents that read my diary will sit down and talk to their children about abuse. Explain to them what is a good touch and what is a bad touch. Don't let your children live with what I must live the rest of my life with. Being sexually abused is a life sentence of memories that can never be erased.

The Elizabeth Smart case was a rare case that got national attention. It was so rare because sexual perpetrators usually don't break in your house and take your children. They are people you know, love, trust with your kids, and sometimes, like in my case, they are family. Don't let your children become victims.

The days of playing with Barbie dolls, chasing the ice cream truck down the street, having lemonade stands, running round in the sprinkler, and playing at the park are of my innocence. I will hold on to them and treasure that part of my childhood.

Tonight as I look up at the stars I pray for all the innocent children in the world. Wherever you are, may God be with you and protect you. Good night and God Bless!

Erin

Epilogue

It's been six months since my book was published. I have received letters from around the country from people touched and moved by my diary. Even more important are the people that have come to me and told me that they are talking to their children. My message is spreading and that is exactly what I wanted to do. I may not have been able to save my own childhood, but the thought of saving another child is what keeps me going.

I contacted the detective who handled our case about a month after my book was published. I spoke with him for about an hour on the phone, and he filled me in on some of my many unanswered questions. I asked the detective how he got Brian to admit. He began by interrogating Brian for three hours. He then gained Brian's trust by telling him that what he did was normal. Eventually Brian started sharing details and, after awhile, the detective had heard enough to tell Brian what he did was illegal.

The detective said that in all his years of work he has never had so many concerned relatives call him about the case. My uncle, who is a cop in our area, tried to use his power to get my cousin off on charges. It made me sick. Brian's mother tried saying my mom brainwashed Allie and I with stories of abuse from her childhood. I couldn't believe so many family members wanted to protect Brian; it made me sick. In the end, Brian received 180 days supervision and short-term counseling which consisted of three visits to a counselor. I guess that is what shocks me. Brian walked away with 180 days supervision and my sister and I are left with a life sentence of memories that can never be erased.

Soon after my book was published, newspapers began to contact me. *The Chicago Tribune* published a story on my book. Soon after, my local paper wrote an article that landed in the homes of many of my relatives. Now Brian's parents won't even look at me or my parents. They are very angry with me and show it. I have other relatives that refuse to speak with me as well. I do not hate my relatives; they just can't handle what happened so they'd rather be upset with me. I've needed to step away from the family and find healthier relationships where I am wanted and accepted. For years I looked for belonging; now I realize I don't belong there and I can do better for myself.

Many wonder what was Brian's reaction when my book was published. I sent him an e-mail informing him of the book and that my intentions are not to get back at him, but to help others. His response surprised me once again.

Erin

I appreciate you telling me and for changing the names in the book. That is very impressive that your book is published. You could have a prominent writing career on your hands. I hope that your book can help a lot of people. Good luck with that.

Brian

Are these the words of a man who held me down and locked me in rooms as a child? Is this the man who threatened me if I told? I feel there is a higher power working through Brian to help him make better choices in life and hold him accountable for his actions. Although I would never trust Brian with a child, I do trust God will watch over Brian and lead him in the right direction in life. If I were to run into Brian today on the streets, I would say hello and go on my way. I am moving on with my life.

I'm now away at college getting my degree in social work. Moving out of my hometown and living in a dorm has been the best thing for me. It has given me a fresh start on life and a new journey. For the first time ever, I'm able to focus in class and be successful. On October 14th, 2004 I will be standing up on stage on my college football field giving a speech to thousands about being a survivor of sexual abuse. For the event, "Take Back the Night," survivors of sexual violence will march through the campus all the way into town.

It will be a very moving experience for me. A year ago at this time I was in a hospital wanting to end my life. A year later I am standing on a stage in front of thousands using the voice that was silenced for so long and speaking out. I am a **Survivor!**

Life Is A Journey

Life is a journey through many terrain
From gardens of pleasure to deserts of pain.
From an ocean of love to a jungle of hate
From mountains of glory to canyons of fate.
There's a highway for joy and a highway for sorrow
A road for today and a road for tomorrow.
So choose your path wisely and walk with care
If you follow your heart you'll find your way there.
I've been to the garden and planted seeds there
I've been to the desert and felt the despair
I swam in the ocean and drank of its wine
I've done all these things since you were mine.
I climbed up the mountain to touch the sky
I went to the canyon and started to cry.
I've traveled both highways, both today and tomorrow
I've basked in the joy and wallowed in sorrow.
My path has been chosen and I walk it with care
I've followed my heart and I'm on my way there.
So I'll just keep on walking till I find what I'm after
To mountains and oceans and gardens of laughter.

—Author Unknown